GW01458639

1913 Diary of Grand Duchess Maria Nikolaevna:

Complete Tercentennial Journal of the Third Daughter of the Last Tsar

Helen Azar

with

Amanda Madru

Copyright © 2017 Helen Azar

All rights reserved.

ISBN: 1546657487
ISBN-13: 978-1546657484

CONTENTS

ACKNOWLEDGEMENTS

Helen Azar would like to thank the following people for their incredible support:

Pierre Hollis, Martin Kalyniuk, Jennifer Eremeeva, Nick Nicholson, Susan Jane Golding, Ben Abajian, Lynn Weddington Tucker, Adam Barnett , Bill Ford, Maureen Greer, James Fody, Valerie-Anne Lutz, Laura Mabee , Kaye Haggerty, Roy Tomlin, Joseph D'Urso, Mary Breheny, Sarai Porretta , John Carnovsky, Bruce Parker, Simonette Carter, Anne Nevala, Hombeline Saclier, Frederick Edward Rehfeldt , Adele Chatelain, Bill Ford, Ann Orth, Eva McDonald, Katrina Kitchen, Heather Drinkwater, Erik Westervelt, Dominic Albanese, Alena Dufkova, Claus Cristian Hansen, Erika Lindblom, Nadieszda Kizenko, Martin Bosch, Nadja Muller, Jillian Armenante, Susan Howl, Valerie Carlsen, Roberta Zisman, Janet Rasmussen, Alex Bender, Janilyn Kocher, Chris Johnson, Gloria DeFalco, Jackie Schweitzer, George Hawkins, Stacy Rubin, Mary Breheny, Yasmin Harris, and last but not least - the wonderful staff at GARF (State Archives of the Russian Federation).

Amanda Madru would like to thank her family: Matt, Laurie, and Lindsay.

GRAND DUCHESS MARIA NIKOLAEVNA'S DIARY

The year 1913 was significant in the saga of Russia's last

Imperial Family, for it marked 300 years since the first

Romanov tsar was crowned. This momentous historical

event was commemorated by a seemingly endless round of

festivities, including parades and processions though

cheering throngs in St. Petersburg, galas for which

traditional court dress was the uniform du jour, and

beginning in May, by a tour of the country—a grand

1

pilgrimage—as Emperor Nicholas II and his family followed the route taken by their ancestor, Mikhail Feodorovich Romanov, to his coronation in the ancient city of Moscow. These events were perhaps the high point of Nicholas's troubled reign, and just over a year later, Archduke Franz Ferdinand, the heir to the Austro-Hungarian throne, would be assassinated at Sarajevo, precipitating the war that would change the face of the world forever.

During this last summer of peace—the last summer of life as it had always been—Grand Duchess Maria Nikolaevna (1899-1918) turned fourteen. The third child of Nicholas II and his wife, Empress Alexandra Feodorovna, is still perhaps the most overlooked of the four Imperial daughters. Her birth was a disappointment for a family and a nation desperate for a son and heir, and her placid nature, along with her position as the middle child, led others to sometimes take her presence for granted: during her brief lifetime, her elder sisters, and of course her only brother, the sickly Heir, were more well-known than she, and it is her younger sister, Anastasia, that history remembers best.

Olga and Tatiana, the two eldest grand duchesses, were known within the family circle as "the Big Pair," whilst Maria and Anastasia were "the Little Pair." Each Pair shared a room, usually wore variations of the same dress, and spent much of their time together—in her diary, Maria makes frequent mention of sharing tea and meals with Anastasia—but while she comprised one half of the Little Pair, and the two were undoubtedly devoted to each other, Maria may have occasionally felt left out due to Anastasia's close bond with their brother, Alexei. In spite of the warm, loving family atmosphere in which she was raised, it is not difficult to imagine that, as the middle child and third girl, Maria may have sometimes felt excluded by her elder sisters, as well as by Anastasia and Alexei, and that she, on occasion, feared she was not as loved as the other children.

Nevertheless, this sweet, affectionate girl who longed to marry a soldier and have twenty children was a buxom, apple-cheeked "Russian beauty" with luxurious light brown hair and large, brilliant blue eyes to which her family referred as "Marie's saucers." Indeed, her father's aunt, Grand Duchess Maria Alexandrovna of Saxe-Coburg-Gotha, once likened her to one of Botticelli's angels. She was

3

renowned for her simplicity and almost angelic kindness, and later, during the dark days of the Revolution, she would become her family's great pillar of strength.

Maria was charming, flirtatious, and merry, but she was also unaffected and genuine. Although she was born into unbelievable wealth, imperial titles and social status meant little to her, and she took great interest in the lives of "ordinary" people, including soldiers, sailors, and servants. Because Nicholas and Alexandra wished their children to be brought up as simply as possible given their remarkable circumstances, even servants addressed Maria by her first name and patronym, Maria Nikolaevna, or by the Russian nickname of "Mashka." She was sincere in her concern for others and utterly devoid of pretension, and these qualities won her the love and admiration of all who knew her.

Like the rest of her family, Maria kept a diary throughout her life. For nearly a century, it was believed that only her 1916 diary survived, but it has recently been discovered that a few others, including this one, also exist. The original letters and diaries of the Romanov family have been preserved by the State Archives of the Russian Federation (GARF) in Moscow, but now, for the first time, Maria's diary has been translated into English, and it has never been seen before by non-specialists.

In her 1913 diary, Maria documents her day-to-day life—visits with her relatives, teatime with friends, religious services, French lessons, and summer fun on board the family's yacht. She records the events of the tercentennial celebrations, noting each city she visited on the provincial tour, and she describes the elaborate Russian gowns that she and her sisters wore to official court functions. She writes fondly of the parties she attended at the St. Petersburg residence of her beloved "Aunt Olga" (Grand Duchess Olga Alexandrovna, Nicholas II's younger sister), and she notes her viewing of various, plays, cinematographs, and ballets. She details going sledding with her father and sisters, and breaking ice on the pond in the Alexander Park at Tsarskoe Selo. Her experiences, although at times steeped in privilege, are surprisingly ordinary.

Maria's diary, which could be read on its own or as a companion to her sister Olga's 1913 journal, is more of a daily log than personal musings and ruminations, but it is her own account of a seminal year in the history of Imperial Russia, and indeed, in the history of the world. She was witness to many key events that would shape the twentieth century and beyond, and her unique perspective is certain to fascinate the casual reader as well as the more expert Romanov aficionado.

Although the teenaged Maria would be brutally murdered by revolutionaries—along with her immediate family and four loyal retainers—a mere five years after this diary was written, her memory lives on in countless black and white photographs, memoirs of those who knew her well, and now, for the first time, in her very own words.

"M.N." Grand Duchess Maria Nikolaevna's initials, written in her own hand.

JANUARY, 1913

1 Tuesday. In the morning went to obednya.[1] Had breakfast with Papa and Sergei.[2] In the afternoon took a walk with Papa then went to Countess Hendrikova, Aunt Mops[3] and to Anya's,[4] where Nikolai Pavlovich[5] was. Had tea with Papa and Mama. Had dinner with Anya.

2 Wednesday. In the morning went to obednya. Had breakfast with Papa, Aunt Olga, Aunt Ksenia[6] and Irina.[7] In the afternoon took a walk with Papa, Aunt Olga and Irina.

---

[1] Holy Liturgy.

[2] Grand Duke Sergei Mikhailovich, one of the Imperial cousins (?).

[3] Evegenia Maximilianovna, Duchess of Leuchtenberg. Mother of "Uncle Petya" and mother-in-law of Grand Duchess Olga Alexandrovna.

[4] Anna Alexandrovna Vyrubova, close friend of the Imperial family.

[5] Nikolai Pavlovich Sablin, the tsar's aide-de-camp.

[6] Grand Duchess Ksenia Alexandrovna, the tsar's sister.

[7] Princess Irina Alexandrovna, daughter of Grand Duchess Ksenia. Maria's first cousin.

Had tea with Papa, Mama and Irina. Had dinner with Papa and Irina.

3 Thursday. Took a ride in the morning, had breakfast with Papa. In the afternoon slid down the hill near the regimental church[8] and then near the white tower.[9] Had tea with Papa and Mama. Had dinner with Anastasia upstairs.

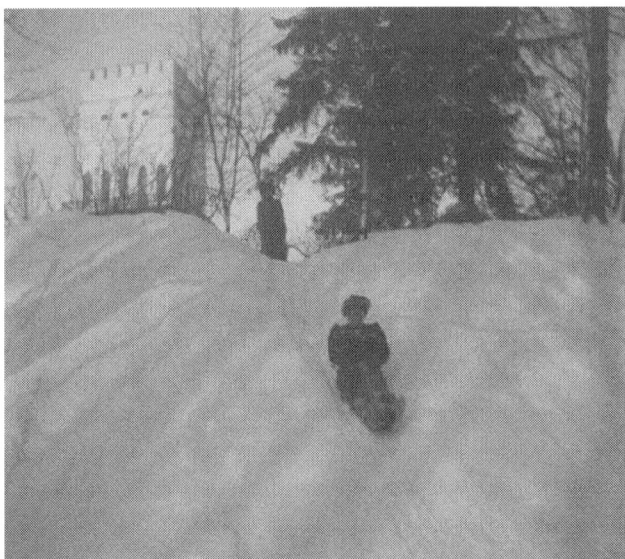

"Sledding.... near the White Tower."

4 Friday. In the morning took a ride with Trina.[10] Had breakfast with Papa and Dunbadze. In the afternoon took a

---

[8] Cathedral at Tsarskoe Selo.
[9] A Gothic-style pavilion in the park of the Alexander Palace.
[10] Catherine Adolphovna Schneider friend and Russian tutor of the Empress.

walk with Papa. Had tea with Papa and Mama. Had dinner upstairs with Anastasia.

5 Saturday. In the morning went to obednya. Had breakfast with Papa and Aunt Olga. Had tea with Papa, Mama and Aunt Olga. Went to vsenoshnaya.[11] Had dinner with Papa, Mama and Aunt Olga.

6 Sunday. In the morning went to obednya. The four of us had breakfast. Anastasia and I took a ride with Trina and then went to the nanny school.[12] Had tea with Mama and Anya. Had dinner upstairs with Anastasia.

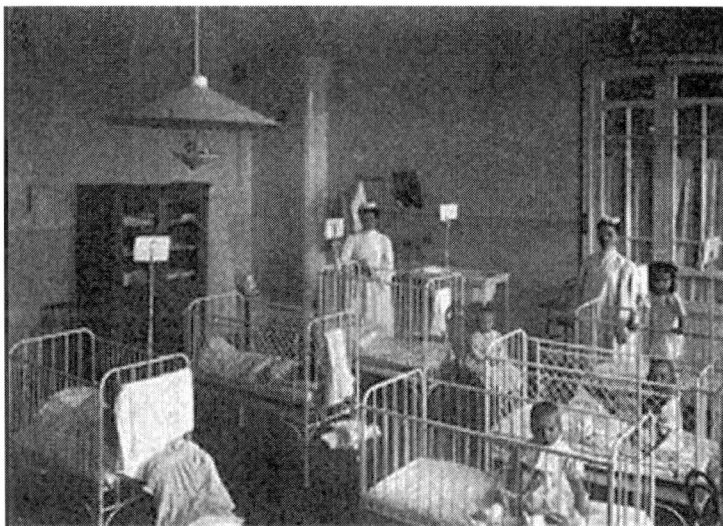

Inside the nanny school

---

[11] Evening services, the all-night vigil.
[12] The Nanny School Of Tsarskoe Selo was an orphanage where future nannies got their training.

7 Monday. In the morning the lessons started. Had breakfast with Papa, Mama and Aunt Minnie. In the afternoon took a walk with Papa. Then went to the officers' yolka.[13] Aunt Olga gave out gifts. Had tea with Papa, Mama and Aunt Olga. Had dinner upstairs with Anastasia.

8 Tuesday. Had lessons in the morning. Four had breakfast with Papa and Uncle Pavel.[14] In the afternoon took a walk with Papa. Then we did exercises. Had tea upstairs with Trina and then went to the dance lesson. Had dinner upstairs with Anastasia.

9 Wednesday. Had lessons in the morning. Had breakfast four with Papa. In the afternoon we took a walk with Papa. Had tea with Papa and Mama. Before dinner played with Trina's Sonia. Had dinner upstairs with Anastasia.

10 Thursday. Had lessons in the morning. Had breakfast four with Papa and Veselkin.[15] While [we were] waiting for Papa, we took a walk to the hill and slid down from it on shovels. Had gymnastics then had tea with Trina. Anastasia and I had a dance [lesson] then I had a music lesson. I had dinner upstairs with Anastasia.

---

[13] Literally translates as "fir tree," Russian meaning is Christmas or New Year party.
[14] Grand Duke Pavel Alexandrovich, uncle to the tsar.
[15] Mikhail Mikhailovich Veselkin

11 Friday. In the morning had lessons. Had breakfast four with Papa, General [illeg] and Kostya.[16] In the afternoon slid down the hill four with Papa. Had music [lesson]. Had tea with Papa, Mama and Alexei, then had a French language lesson. We had dinner four with Mama. Papa had dinner with Cuirassier regiment for monthly dinner.

12 Saturday. In the morning went to molebna.[17] Had breakfast four with Papa, Aunt Olga and Sashka.[18] In the afternoon we slid down the hill with Papa, Aunt Olga and Sashka. Had tea five with Papa, Mama, Aunt Olga and Irina. Went to vsenoshnaya with Papa and Irina at the regiment church. Had dinner four with Papa, Irina, Sashka and [illeg].

---

[16] Prince Konstantin Konstantinovich, third son of Grand Duke Konstantin Konstantinovich.
[17] Intercessory prayer service.
[18] One of the suite officers, possibly Alexander Shvedov

"Aunt Olga."

13 Sunday. In the morning went to obednya at the regiment church. There was a breakfast with the officers. I sat with K. Egorovich and Prince Kochubei. In the afternoon stayed home because I have a cold. Had tea with Mama and Papa. Got dressed and went to the theatre. At dinner in the train I sat with Dedulin and Stefanovich. There was a ballet "Little Hunchbacked Horse." On the way back we had tea in the train, I sat with Dedulin and Prince Orlov.

14 Monday. Had lessons in the morning. Had breakfast four. In the afternoon stayed home and read with Trina. Had tea with Papa and Mama. Did homework. Had dinner with Anastasia.

15 Tuesday. Had lessons in the morning. Had breakfast four with Papa, Aunt Olga and Uncle Petya[19]. Stayed home during the day. Madame [illeg] came by. Had tea with Papa, Mama, Aunt Olga and Uncle Petya. Had a music lesson and then did homework. Had dinner with Anastasia.

16 Wednesday. Had lessons in the morning. Had breakfast four. In the afternoon stayed home and sat with Mama and Anya. Then had a music lesson. Had tea with Papa, Mama and Alexei. Did homework. Went to Trina's. Had dinner with Anastasia.

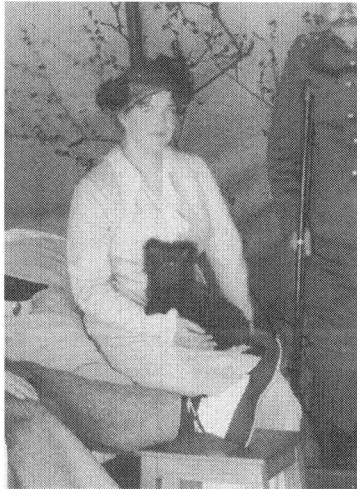

Maria holding Anastasia's pet dog, Shvybzik.

---

[19] Duke Peter Alexandrovich of Oldenburg. First husband of Grand Duchess Olga Alexandrovna.

17 Thursday. Had lessons in the morning. Had breakfast with Papa and Hessians. In the afternoon stayed home and looked at books. Had tea with Mama and Papa. Had a music [lesson]. Did homework, then went to Trina's. Had dinner with Mama, Anastasia and Anya.

18 Friday. Had lessons in the morning. Had breakfast four with Papa. In the afternoon stayed home and sat with Mama and Anya. Had tea with Papa, Mama and Alexei. Before that had a music lesson. After that, Anastasia and I had French reading. Then did homework. Had dinner with Anastasia.

19 Saturday. In the morning four had breakfast with Papa, Aunt Olga and Fabritzky.[20] In the afternoon took a walk with Papa and Aunt Olga. Had tea with Mama, Papa and Aunt Olga. Went to camp church with Papa and Aunt Olga. Had dinner with Anastasia.

20 Sunday. Went to obednya at the regiment church. At breakfast sat with Prince Kochubei and Count Benkendorf.[21] Went to the city with A. E. to Grandmama's,[22] from there went to Aunt Olga's. Played, had tea and dinner, Irina,

---

[20] Rear-admiral Semyon Semyonovich Fabritzky.
[21] Count Alexander Konstantinovich Benkendorf was ambassador to Denmark and the United Kingdom.
[22] Dowager Empress Maria Feodorovna, mother of the tsar.

[illeg], Andrei,[23] [illeg] and her mother, Sablin,[24] Voronov,[25] Rodionov,[26] [illeg], Kulikovsky,[27] Khvoshinsky, Klyucharev. From there went to a ballet with Papa. It was "Don Quixote," returning in the train we had tea, I sat with [illeg] and Dedulin.

The imperial entrance of the regiment church, aka Feodorovsky Cathedral.

21 Monday. Had lessons in the morning. Had breakfast four with Papa and Mama on the sofa. In the afternoon

---

[23] Prince Andrei Alexandrovich, son of Grand Duchess Ksenia Alexandrovna.
[24] Nikolai Sablin, also known by nickname "Kiki"
[25] Pavel Alexeyevich Voronov
[26] Nikolai Nikolaevich Rodionov.
[27] Nikolai Nikolaevich Kulikovsky, who would eventually become the second husband of Grand Duchess Olga Alexandrovna.

took a walk with Papa. I had a music lesson. Had tea with Papa and Mama. Then did homework. Had dinner with Anastasia.

22 Tuesday. Had lessons in the morning. Had breakfast four with Trina and Mama on the sofa. In the afternoon took a walk with Papa. Had tea with Trina. Had a dance lesson. Then had a music lesson. Then did homework. Had dinner with Anastasia.

23 Wednesday. Had lessons in the morning. Had breakfast four with Mama on the sofa. In the afternoon slid down the hill. Trina was with us. Had a music lesson. Had tea with Mama and Papa. Then did homework. Had dinner with Anastasia.

24 Thursday. Had lessons in the morning. Had breakfast four with Papa and Mama on the sofa. In the afternoon took a walk with Papa. Drove to Petersburg to Aunt Ksenia's, from there to Grandmama's, there we had tea and there was a yolka. Had dinner with Aunt Olga, Papa, Uncle Petya, Andrei, Oleg,[28] Nikita[29] and we four. Returned.

25 Friday. Had lessons in the morning. Had breakfast four with Mama on the sofa. Slid down the hill with Papa. Had a music lesson. Had tea with Mama and Papa. Anastasia and

---

[28] Prince Oleg Konstantinovich, fourth son of Grand Duke Konstantin Konstantinovich.
[29] Prince Nikita Alexandrovich, son of Grand Duchess Ksenia Alexandrovna. Maria's first cousin.

I had French reading [lesson]. Had dinner upstairs with Anastasia.

26 Saturday. Had lessons in the morning. Had breakfast four with Papa, Aunt Olga and Mama on the sofa. In the afternoon took a walk with Papa and Aunt Olga. Had tea four with Mama, Papa and Aunt Olga. Went to vsenoshnaya at the regiment church. Had dinner four with Papa, Aunt Olga and Mama on the sofa.

27 Sunday. In the morning to obednya at the regiment church. At breakfast sat with Dedulin and [blank space]. In the afternoon took a walk with Papa. Had tea with Irina, Feodor,[30] Rostislav,[31] Georgiy[32] and R[illeg]. Then we went to [see] a cinematograph. Had dinner with Anastasia and Alexei.

28 Monday. Had lessons in the morning. Had breakfast four with Mama on the sofa. In the afternoon Trina went with to the hill to slide down. Had a music lesson. Had tea with Mama and Papa. Then did homework. Had dinner with Papa, Count [illeg] and Mama on the sofa.

29 Tuesday. Had lessons in the morning. Had breakfast four with Papa, Nikolai Pavlovich and Mama on the sofa.

---

[30] Prince Feodor Alexandrovich, son of Grand Duchess Ksenia Alexandrovna.
[31] Prince Rostislav Alexandrovich, son of Grand Duchess Ksenia Alexandrovna.
[32] Prince Georgiy Konstantinovich, youngest son of Grand Duke Konstantin Konstantinovich.

Had tea upstairs with Trina. Had a dance lesson then music. Did homework. Had dinner with Anastasia.

30 Wednesday. Had lessons in the morning. Had breakfast four with Mama on the sofa. In the afternoon Trina came with us to the hill and we slid down there. Had tea with Mama and Papa. Had music lesson, then did homework. Had dinner with Anastasia, Anya and Mama on the sofa.

OTMA with "Anya" Vyrubova.

31 Thursday. Had lessons in the morning. Had breakfast four with Anya and Mama on the sofa. In the afternoon Trina went with us to the hill--we slid there. Had tea upstairs with Trina. Had a dance lesson. Had a music lesson. Then did homework. Had dinner with Anastasia.

~

FEBRUARY, 1913

1 Friday. Had lessons in the morning. Had breakfast four with Papa and Mama on the sofa. In the afternoon walked to the hill with Trina. Had a music lesson. Had tea with Trina. Anastasia and I had French reading lesson. Four went to the regiment church. Had dinner four with Papa and Mama on the sofa.

2 Saturday. Went to obednya with Papa and Aunt Olga. Had breakfast four with Papa, Aunt Olga and Mama on the sofa. Took a walk and slid down the hill with Papa and Aunt Olga. Had tea with Mama, Papa and Aunt Olga. Went to vsenoshnaya with Papa and Aunt Olga. Had dinner four with Papa, Aunt Olga and Mama on the sofa. Then four with Papa, Mama and Aunt Olga to [illeg], there were both Dehns,[33] Sablin, Rodionov, Butakov, Zlebov and Kazhevnikov. There was a ventriloquist and then [they] played.

---

[33] Yulia "Lili" Dehn - lady in waiting, and her sister-in-law, Sonia.

Maria in the snow with "Papa," "Aunt Olga," her sisters, and officers.

3 Sunday. Went four to obednya. Had breakfast four with Mama on the sofa. In the afternoon slid down the hill with Papa. Had tea five with Dmitri, Rostislav and Vasili.[34] Then we went to a cinematograph. Went to the theatre. At dinner in the train sat with Prince Trubetzkoy[35] and Minevich.

---

[34] Sons of Grand Duchess Ksenia Alexandrovna.
[35] Prince Nikolai Sergeyevich Trubetzkoy, a Russian linguist and historian at court.

4 Monday. Lessons in the morning. Had breakfast four with Papa, Mama and Petrovsky. In the afternoon slid down the hill with Papa. Had music lesson. Had tea with Papa and Mama. Then did homework. Had dinner with Anastasia.

5 Tuesday. Had lessons in the morning. Had breakfast four with Papa, Mama and Kostya. In the afternoon slid down the hill with Papa. Mama [was] with Anya and Apraksin. Had tea with Trina. Had a dance lesson. Had a music lesson. Then did homework. Had dinner with Anastasia.

6 Wednesday. Had lessons in the morning. Had breakfast four with Mama and Madame Zizi.[36] In the afternoon sledded near White Tower with Papa and Anya. Alexei was there too. Had a music lesson. Had tea with Papa and Mama. Then did homework. Had dinner with Anastasia.

7 Thursday. Rode around with Anastasia and Madame Conrad.[37] Then had lessons. Had breakfast four with Mama and Anya. In the afternoon sledded near white tower. Alexei was there too. Had tea with Trina. Had a music [crossed out] dance lesson, then music. Then did homework. Had dinner with Anastasia.

---

[36] Elizaveta Alexeyevna Naryshkina, mistress of the robes.
[37] Wife of the music teacher to the Imperial children.

Maria in 1913.

8 Friday. Had lessons in the morning. Had breakfast four with Papa, Mama and Uncle Georgiy.[38] In the afternoon sledded with Anya near the white tower. Mama and Alexei were there too. Had a music lesson. Had tea with Mama and Papa. Anastasia and I had French reading. Then did homework. Anastasia and I had dinner with Mama on the sofa.

9 Saturday. Had lessons in the morning. Had breakfast four with Papa, Mama, Aunt Olga and Pogulyaev. In the afternoon sledded near the white tower with Papa, Aunt

---

[38] Grand Duke Georgiy Mikhailovich, one of the Imperial cousins.

Olga, Pogulyaev and Anya. Mama and Alexei were there too. Had tea with Mama, Papa, Aunt Olga and Aunt Ksenia. Went to vsenoshnaya at the regiment church with Papa, Mama and Aunt Olga. Had dinner four with Papa, Mama, Aunt Olga and Pogulyaev.

10 Sunday. In the morning went to obednya with Papa at the regiment church. At breakfast sat with Gavril[39] and Drenteln.[40] Went to Petersburg to Grandmama's from there to Aunt Olga's. Played, had tea and dinner. There were: Irina, Andrusha,[41] Feodor, Sasha, Nadya and their mama, Zoya, Khvoshinsky, Klyucharev, Rodionov, Count Ungengiterberg, Skvortzov, Shvedov[42], Kulikovsky and Isan[illeg]. At dinner sat with Skvotzov and Shangin. Then [we] went to the circus with the Cossacks, Nadya, Klyucharev, Kulikovsky, Prince Gagarin[43] and Lili.[44]

11 Monday. In the morning I stayed in bed. Had breakfast four with Papa, Sergei and Mama on the sofa. In the afternoon I stayed home and Trina read. Had a music lesson. Had tea with Papa and Mama. Did homework. Had dinner with Anastasia.

---

[39] Prince Gavril Konstantinovich, second son of Grand Duke Konstantin Konstantinovich.
[40] Alexander Alexandrovich Drenteln, the tsar's Major-General.
[41] Nickname for Maria's cousin Prince Andrei Alexandrovich.
[42] See "Sashka".
[43] Prince Nicholas Gagarin.
[44] Yulia Dehn, the wife of an officer at court and friend to the empress.

12 Tuesday. Had lessons in the morning. Had breakfast four with Papa, Aunt Olga, Uncle Petya and Mama on the sofa. In the afternoon I stayed home and Trina read. Had tea with Papa, Mama, Aunt Olga and Uncle Petya. Had a music lesson. Did homework. Had dinner with Anastasia.

13 Wednesday. Had lessons in the morning. Had breakfast four with Anya and Mama on the sofa. In the afternoon sledded with Olga and Tatiana. Had a music lesson. Had tea with Papa and Mama. Then did homework. Had dinner with Anastasia.

Maria with "Papa" and Olga.

14 Thursday. In the morning sledded with Anastasia and Madame Conrad. Then had lessons. Had breakfast four with Mama on the sofa. In the afternoon sledded with Olga and Trina. Had tea with Mama. Went to a cinematograph, there were four little [illeg]. Had a music lesson. Then did homework. Had dinner with Anastasia.

15 Friday. Had lessons in the morning. Had breakfast four with Mama on the sofa. In the afternoon sledded near the white tower with Papa. Had tea with Mama and Papa. Before tea had a music lesson. Then Anastasia and I had French reading. Did homework. Had dinner with Anastasia.

16 Saturday. Had lessons in the morning. Had breakfast four with Papa, Aunt Olga, Aunt Ella[45] and Mama on the sofa. In the afternoon took a walk with Papa and Aunt Olga and then sledded near the white tower. Had tea with Mama, Papa, Aunt Olga and Aunt Ella. Went to the regiment church for vsenoshnaya with Papa, Aunt Olga and Aunt Ella. Then there was a cinematograph. They showed historical films.

17 Sunday. In the morning went to obednya at the regiment church with Aunt Ella. Had breakfast four with Papa, Aunt Ella, Ivanchik[46] and Mama on the sofa. Drove to

---

[45] Grand Duchess Elizaveta Feodorovna, widow of Grand Duke Sergei Alexandrovich. Aunt-by-marriage to the tsar and sister to the empress
[46] Prince Ioann Konstantinovich, eldest son of Grand Duke Konstantin Konstantinovich.

Petersburg to Grandmama's from there to Aunt Olga's. Played and had tea. There were: Irina, Andrei, Feodor, Sasha, Nadya, their brother and their mama, Zoya, Rodionov, Klyucharev, Count Ungershterberg, Shvedov, Fedushkin, Kulikovsky, Shemzin, Zarnakaz, Kulnev.

18 Monday. Had lessons in the morning. Had breakfast four with Aunt Ella and Mama on the sofa. In the afternoon slid down the hill and near the white tower with Papa. Had tea alone. Then had a music [lesson]. Then did homework. Had dinner with Anastasia.

19 Tuesday. Had lessons in the morning. Had breakfast four with Papa, Aunt Ella and Mama on the sofa. In the afternoon drove to Petersburg. First we went to the Savior[47] and then home to the palace. Had tea with Anastasia and Alexei, had dinner with them too.

20 Wednesday. In the morning all four sledded with Trina. Had breakfast four with Papa, Aunt Ella and Drenteln. Stayed home in the afternoon. Had tea with Mama, Papa and Aunt Olga. Before tea, Grandmama stopped by Mama's. Had dinner four with Aunt Ella and Mama on the sofa.

21 Thursday. In the morning took a walk in the park. Then drove to Kazansky Cathedral for molebna. Had breakfast four with Papa, Grandmama and Aunt Olga. In the

---

[47] Church of Christ the Savior

afternoon we were all in Russian dresses[48] and there was a "baise main."[49] Had tea at the children's monastery with Anastasia.

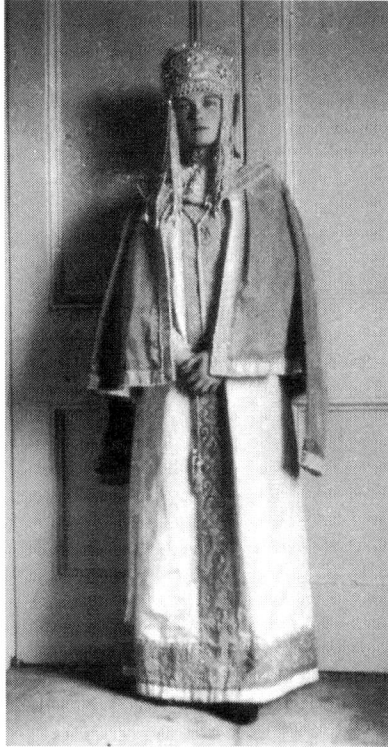

Grand Duchess Olga in "Russian dress."

22 Friday. In the morning took a walk [crossed out] there was a "baise main." Had breakfast with Papa, Grandmama,

---

[48] Embroidered Russian court gowns
[49] Ritual kissing of hands

Aunt Olga, Aunt Ksenia and Uncle Petya. In the afternoon took a walk with Papa and Alexei. Had tea with Alexei and four little Ai Todortzy. Had dinner with Papa. Took a bath with Mama in the bathtub.

23 Saturday. In the morning took a walk with Papa. Then there was a "baise main" for the ladies. Had breakfast with Papa and Grandmama. In the afternoon took a walk with Papa. Had tea with all the Ai Todortzy. Went to Trina's. Had dinner with Olga and Papa. Anastasia and I took a bath in the big bathtub at Papa's. Tatiana has typhus.

24 Sunday. In the morning went to obednya with Papa. Had breakfast with Papa. In the afternoon went to Aunt Olga's there we had tea, played. At her [place] were: Irina, Andrusha, Sasha, Nadya, Kolya and their mama, Count Ungermeterberg, Shvedov, Yuzik, Skvortzov, Sablin, Klyucharev, Kulikovsky, Zarnekoy, Zoya, [illeg]. Had dinner with Anastasia.

25 Monday. In the morning went to church. Had breakfast with Papa, Uncle Boris,[50] Tatiana and Bagration.[51] Took a walk with Papa on the roof and in the garden. Had tea with Mama and Anya. Went to church. Had dinner with Papa and Bagration. Took a bath in Papa's bathtub. Mama, Papa and Aunt Olga watched.

---

[50] Grand Duke Boris Vladimirovich, cousin of the tsar.
[51] Princess Tatiana Konstantinovna, eldest daughter of Grand Duke Konstantin Konstantinovich, and her husband Prince Konstantin Bagration-Mukhransky.

"...in the garden."

26 Tuesday. In the morning went to church with Papa. Had breakfast with Papa and Uncle Pavel. In the afternoon drove to Tsarskoe Selo. Had tea downstairs with Mama and Papa. Went to church with Papa. Had dinner with Papa and Mama on the sofa.

27 Wednesday. In the morning went to church with Papa. Had breakfast with Papa, Chitkevich and Mama on the sofa. In the afternoon built a tower with snow on the ice rink with Papa. Then there was music. Had tea with Mama and Papa. Went to church with Papa. Had dinner with Papa and Mama on the sofa.

Maria dressed in furs.

28 Thursday. In the morning went to church with Papa. Had breakfast with Papa, Count Grabbe[52] and Mama on the sofa. In the afternoon built a tower with Papa. Had tea alone. Then had a music lesson. Went to church with Papa, Mama and Alexei. Had dinner with Papa, Count Grabbe and Mama on the sofa.

~

---

[52] Count Alexander Grabbe, aide-de-camp to the tsar.

MARCH, 1913

1 Friday. In the morning sledded with Madame Conrad.
Went to church with Papa, Mama and Alexei. Had breakfast
with Papa, Sablin and Mama on the sofa. In the afternoon
made a tower with Papa and Sablin. Had tea with Mama
and Papa. Confessed. Went to church with Papa, Sablin
and Mama on the sofa [sic].

2 Saturday. In the morning had Communion. Then had tea
with Mama and Papa. Had breakfast with Mama on the
sofa, Papa and Count Fredericks.[53] In the afternoon took
and walk and made the tower with Papa and Aunt Olga.
Had tea with Papa, Mama and Aunt Olga. Went to Svodny
church[54] with Papa, Aunt Olga and Mama on the sofa.

---

[53] Count Vladimir Borisovich Fredericks, the Imperial household
minister.
[54] The church of the Svodny regiment.

3 Sunday. In the morning went to the regiment church. Had breakfast with Anya and Mama on the sofa. In the afternoon took a walk. Had tea and played with 4 little Ai Todortzy,[55] Vera and Georgiy. Had dinner with Anastasia, Alexei and little Ai Todortzy.

4 Monday. Had lessons in the morning. Had breakfast with Papa and Mama on the sofa. Went to the review of the Albavsky sailors. Had tea alone. Had a music lesson. Went to Realnoe school[56] with Olga and Trina for a physics [lesson]. Did homework. Had dinner with Anastasia and Alexei.

Realnoe School, circa 1913

5 Tuesday. In the morning sledded with Madame Conrad. Had lessons. Had breakfast with Mama on the sofa. In the afternoon stayed home due to a cold. We got haircuts and

---

[55] That is, those from Ai Todor.
[56] Realnoe Uchilische (school) was founded by Nicholas II in 1900. The school focused on natural sciences, and the imperial children went there to use laboratory equipment for physics lessons.

Tatiana's got all cut off. Had tea in the playroom. Had dance lessons then did homework. Had dinner with Mama on the sofa.

6 Wednesday. Had lessons in the morning. Had breakfast four with Papa, Fabritzky and Mama on the sofa. In the afternoon stayed home. Had a music lesson. Had tea in the playroom. Did homework. Had dinner with Anastasia. The King of Greece has died.[57]

7 Thursday. In the morning sledded with Madame Conrad, then had lessons. Had breakfast with Papa and Mama on the sofa. In the afternoon took a walk with Papa. Had tea alone, then had a music lesson. Did homework. Went to the lower regiment church.[58] Had dinner with Papa and Mama on the sofa.

---

[57] King George I of Greece, brother of Dowager Empress Maria Feodorovna, was assassinated by an alleged socialist.
[58] The Imperial family's private chapel located in the cellar of the Feodorovsky Cathedral.

Maria studying her lessons.

8 Friday. Had lessons in the morning, then went to the lower regiment church with Olga. Had breakfast with Papa and Mama on the sofa. In the afternoon took a walk with Papa. Had a music lesson. Had tea with Mama and Papa. Anastasia and I had French reading. Did homework. Had dinner with Mama on the sofa.

9 Saturday. Had lessons in the morning. Had breakfast [four - crossed out] with Papa, Aunt Olga, Count Fredericks and Count Irod. In the afternoon sledded with Anastasia and Madame Conrad. Had tea with Mama, Papa and Aunt Olga. Went to the regiment church with Papa and Aunt Olga. Had dinner with Papa, Aunt Olga and Mama on the sofa.

10 Sunday. In the morning went to the regiment church with Papa. Had breakfast with Papa and Mama on the sofa and Prince [illeg]. Went to Petersburg, at first were at Grandmama's and then went to Aunt Olga's. There we had tea and looked at her exhibit. Had dinner upstairs with Anastasia's.

11 Monday. Had lessons in the morning. Had breakfast with Papa and Mama on the sofa. Went to a review. Had tea alone. Had a music lesson. Went to a physics lesson with Olga and Trina. Did homework. Had dinner with Alexei and Anastasia.

12 Tuesday. In the morning sledded with Madame Conrad. Had lessons. Had breakfast with Papa and Mama on the sofa. In the afternoon sledded with Lili. Had a music lesson. Had tea with Mama and Papa. Did homework. Had dinner with Anastasia and Alexei.

13 Wednesday. Had lessons in the morning. Had breakfast with Mama on the sofa. In the afternoon broke the ice with Papa. Had tea alone. Had a music lesson, did homework, then read with Trina. Had dinner with Anastasia and Alexei.

14 Thursday. In the morning sledded with Madame Conrad. Had lessons. Had breakfast with Papa and Mama on the sofa. In the afternoon broke the ice with Papa. Had tea alone. Had a music lesson, then did homework, then read with Trina. Had dinner with Alexei and Anastasia.

15 Friday. Had lessons in the morning. Had breakfast with Papa and Mama on the sofa. In the afternoon broke ice with Papa, Alexei was also there. Had tea alone. Had a music lesson. Anastasia and I had French reading. Did homework. Had dinner with Anastasia and Alexei.

Maria "breaking ice."

16 Saturday. Had lessons in the morning. Had breakfast with Papa, Aunt Olga, Gavril[59] and Count Fredericks. In the afternoon broke ice with Papa, Alexei was also there. Had tea with Mama, Papa and Aunt Olga. Went to vsenoshnaya at the regiment church with Papa and Aunt Olga. Had dinner with Papa, Aunt Olga, Gavril and Mama on the sofa.

---

[59] Prince Gavril Konstantinovich, second son of Grand Duke Konstantin Konstantinovich.

"In the afternoon broke ice with Papa..." Maria and Olga breaking ice with their father in the Alexander Park.

17 Sunday. In the morning went to obednya with Papa at the regiment church. Had breakfast with Papa, Ioann,[60] Gavril and Mama on the sofa. Went to Petersburg, at first to Grandmama's and then to Aunt Olga's, there were: Irina, Andrei, Feodor, Sasha and her mother, Count Ungershternberg, Shvedov,[61] Skvortzev, Yuzik, and Kulikovsky. We played, had tea and dinner and returned home.

---

[60] Prince Ioann Konstantinovich.
[61] Alexander Konstantinovich Shvedov, an officer in the tsar's Escort Guard.

18 Monday. Had lessons in the morning. Had breakfast with Papa, Kostya and Mama on the sofa. Went to a review of the Kronshtadtsky sailors. Then broke the ice with Papa and Alexei. Had tea alone. Had a music lesson. Had dinner with Anastasia and Alexei.

19 Tuesday. In the morning sledded with Madame Conrad. Had lessons. Had breakfast with Papa and Mama on the sofa. In the afternoon broke ice with Papa and Drenteln, Alexei was there too. Had tea alone. Had a music lesson. Did homework. Went to the lower regiment church. Had dinner with Anastasia.

20 Wednesday. Had lessons in the morning. Went to the lower regiment church with Nastenka.[62] Had breakfast with Nastenka and Mama on the sofa. In the afternoon broke ice with Papa, Alexei was there too. Had music [lesson]. Had tea with Papa and Alexei. Did homework. Had dinner with Anastasia and Alexei.

21 Thursday. In the morning sledded with Madame Conrad. Had lessons. Had breakfast with Papa and Mama on the sofa. In the afternoon broke ice with Papa. Had tea alone. Had music [lesson]. Went to the lower regiment church. Had dinner with Papa and Mama on the sofa.

22 Friday. In the morning went to Petersburg with Papa to [see] the artisan exhibit. Had breakfast at Grandmama's

---

[62] Anastasia Vasiliyevna Hendrikova, lady-in-waiting.

with Papa, Aunt Olga, Uncle Petya and Irina. In the afternoon broke ice with Papa. Had a music lesson. Had tea with Papa, Mama and Aunt Miechen's[63] brother. Anastasia and I had French reading then did homework. Had dinner with Anastasia.

23 Saturday. Had lessons in the morning. Had breakfast with Papa, Aunt Olga, Veselkin and Mama on the sofa. Took a walk with Papa and Aunt Olga in the afternoon and broke ice. Had tea with Mama, Papa and Aunt Olga. Went to vsenoshnaya at the regiment church, with Papa and Aunt Olga. Had dinner with Papa, Aunt Olga, Veselkin and Mama on the sofa.

24 Sunday. In the morning went to obednya at the regiment church with Papa. At breakfast sat with Ioann and Komakov. In the afternoon broke ice with Papa and Irina. Had tea with the little Ai Todortzy, Georgiy and Vera, and played. Went to vsenoshnaya with Papa at the regiment church. Had dinner with Papa, Bagration and Mama on the sofa.

25 Monday. In the morning went to Petersburg with Papa. Went to obednya at Anichkov with Grandmama. Had breakfast with Grandmama, Aunt Olga and Irina with [her] brothers. Had tea, played and had dinner at Aunt Olga's. There were: Count Ungershternberg, Shvedov, Yuzik, Skvortzov, Zborovsky, Zarbuchalo, Shangin, Kulikovsky,

---

[63] Grand Duchess Maria Vladimirovna, widow of Grand Duke Vladimir Alexandrovich. Aunt-by-marriage to the tsar.

Felix, Irina with [her] brothers, Sasha with mother, Kolya, Nadya and Uncle Petya. And returned home.

26 Tuesday. Had lessons in the morning. Sledded with Madame Conrad. Had breakfast with Papa and Sergei. In the afternoon broke ice with Papa, Alexei was there too. Had tea with Olga and Anastasia. Had a dance lesson. Had a music lesson. Had dinner with Anastasia and Alexei.

27 Wednesday. Had lessons in the morning. Had breakfast with Olga and Anastasia. In the afternoon broke ice with Papa, Alexei was there too. Had tea alone. Had a music lesson. Went to the physics lesson with Olga and Lili. Did homework. Went to the lower regiment church. Had dinner with Olga and Anastasia.

28 Thursday. In the morning sledded with Madame Conrad. Had one lesson. Went to the manege[64] to a parade of the Svodny regiment with Papa and Aunt Olga. At breakfast sat with Sherikhovsky and Kutepov. In the afternoon took a walk and broke ice with Papa and Aunt Olga. Had tea alone. Anastasia and I had a dance lesson. Had a music lesson. Did homework. Had dinner upstairs with Olga and Anastasia.

[This page had a dried flower in it, marked "A rose from the Svodny regiment from the parade"].

---

[64] An arena or enclosed area where horses and riders are trained. In this case, an indoor riding arena at Tsarskoe Selo.

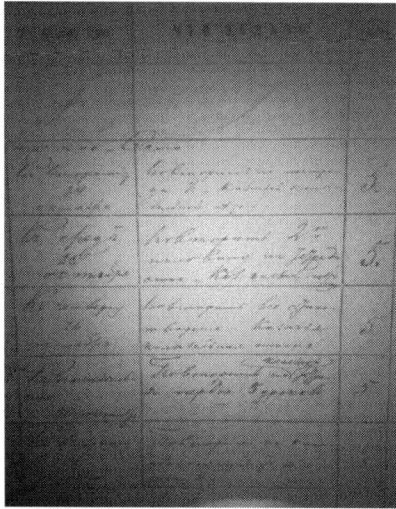

Maria's list of lessons and homework assignment grades. "5"is equivalent to an "A;" we can see that the grand duchess was a very good student.

29 Friday. Had lessons in the morning. Had breakfast with Papa and Uncle Petya. In the afternoon broke ice with Papa. Had music [lesson]. Had tea with Mama, Papa and Uncle Petya. Anastasia and I had French reading. Did homework. Had dinner with Anastasia and Alexei.

30 Saturday. Had lessons in the morning. Had breakfast with Papa, Aunt Olga, Uncle Mitya and Mordvinov. In the afternoon took a walk and broke ice with Papa and Aunt Olga. Had tea with Papa, Mama and Aunt Olga. Went to the regiment church for vsenoshnaya with Papa and Aunt Olga. Had dinner with Papa, Aunt Olga and Dmitri.

31 Sunday. In the morning went to obednya with Papa at the regiment church. At breakfast sat with Count Rostovtzev and Prince Gotgoselsky. Went to Petersburg, at first to Grandmama's, and then to Aunt Olga's. At her [place] we had tea and played. There were: Uncle Petya, Kulikovsky, Count Ungershternberg, Shvedov, Yuzik, Zborovsky, Kolya and mother, Klyucharev and Shangin.

~

APRIL, 1913

1 Monday. Had lessons in the morning. Had breakfast with Papa, Aunt Olga and Mama on the sofa. Went to the review of the guard equipage. Had tea with all the Ai Todortzy. Had a music lesson 20 m. Went to a cinematograph and Vera.[65] Did homework. Had dinner with Anastasia.

2 Tuesday. Rode [in carriage] with Madame Conrad. Had lessons. Had breakfast four with Papa, Uncle Sergei and Mama on the sofa. In the afternoon broke ice with Papa. Had a dance lesson. Went to Petersburg to the [illeg] of Andrei. At dinner sat with Papa and Prince Putyatin and coming back on the train at tea [sat] with Papa and Drenteln.

---

[65] Princess Vera Konstantinovna, youngest daughter of Grand Duke Konstantin Konstantinovich.

3 Wednesday. Had lessons in the morning. Had breakfast four with Papa, Sablin and Mama on the sofa. In the afternoon took a walk and broke ice with Papa and Sablin. Had tea alone. Had a music lesson. Did homework. Had dinner with Anastasia.

4 Thursday. Rode [in carriage] with Madame Conrad. Had lessons. Had breakfast four with Papa, Aunt Olga, Lekhtenberg and Mama on the sofa. In the afternoon took a walk with Aunt Olga and Tatiana [was] in a small carriage as she is still not allowed to walk. Had tea with Anastasia. Had a music lesson. Had dinner with Alexei and Anastasia.

5 Friday. Had lessons in the morning. Had breakfast four with Papa, Arsenov and Mama on the sofa. In the afternoon broke ice with Papa. Had tea alone. Had a music lesson. Studied French with Anastasia. Did homework. Had dinner four with Mama on the sofa.

6 Saturday. Had lessons in the morning. Went four with Papa to a parade of our Cossack regiment. Had breakfast five with Nastenka and Mama on the sofa. In the afternoon broke ice four with Papa. Had tea four with Papa and Mama. Went to vsenoshnaya at the regiment church five with Papa and Mama. Had dinner four with Papa, Count Grabbe and Mama on the sofa.

7 Sunday. In the morning five with Papa went to obednya at the regiment church. At breakfast sat with Komarov and

Count Sheremetiev.[66] In the afternoon rode around with
Trina. Had tea and went to a cinematograph with Ritka,
Irina and [her] brothers. Had dinner 4 with Papa, Irina,
Feodor, Nikita and Mama on the sofa. Looked at the
pictures of Prokudin Gorsky.[67]

8 Monday. In the morning rode around 4 with Madame
Conrad. Had breakfast with Papa and Mama on the sofa. In
the afternoon broke ice 5 with Papa. Had tea 4 with Mama
and Papa. Went to a pre-consecrated obednya 5 with Papa.
Went again to the lower regiment church 5 with Papa. Had
dinner 4 with Papa and Mama on the sofa.

9 Tuesday. In the morning rode around 4 with Madame.
Went 5 with Papa to the pre-consecrated obednya at the
lower church. Had breakfast 5 with Papa and Mama on the
sofa. Broke ice with Papa. Had tea 4 with Mama, Papa,
Aunt Ksenia and Uncle Sandro. Went to church with Papa
and Mama. Had dinner 4 with Papa and Mama on the sofa.

10 Wednesday. Rode with Madame. Went 5 to the lower
regiment [church] with Papa, Mama and Aunt Olga. Had
breakfast 5 with Papa, Aunt Olga and Mama on the sofa.
Went to the garden with Papa and Aunt Olga. Confessed.
Had tea 4 with Papa, Mama and Aunt Olga. Went to church
with Mama and Papa. Had dinner 4 with Mama [sic] and
Mama on the sofa.

---

[66] Count Alexander Sheremetiev.
[67] Sergei Prokudin-Gorsky, chemist and photographer, pioneer of
early color photography.

Maria relaxing in the hammock in the garden.

11 Thursday. In the morning 5 with Papa and Mama took Holy Communion at the lower regiment church. Rode around with Nastenka. Had breakfast 5 with Papa and Mama on the sofa. In the afternoon [took a walk--crossed out] broke ice with Papa. Had tea 4 with Papa and Mama. Went to the 12 Old Testament [readings?] at the large regiment church with Mama and Papa. Had dinner with Papa and Mama on the sofa.

12 Friday. In the morning took a walk with Papa. Had breakfast with Papa and Mama on the sofa. In the afternoon took a walk with Papa and rode little boats. Had

tea 4 with Mama and Papa. Went to Trina's. Had dinner 4 with Papa and Mama on the sofa.

13 Saturday. In the morning at 5 o'clock went to pogrebenie[68] at the regiment church. Had breakfast with Papa and Mama on the sofa. Went to Anya's 4 with Papa and Mama and colored eggs and had tea. There were: Kiki,[69] Isa,[70] Lili, Rodionov, Kozhevnikov and Pi. Had dinner 4 with Papa and Mama. Went 5 with Papa and Mama to zautrenya[71] and then to obednya, and then prepared for communion [Dried flower marker "Lilac from zautrenya from the regiment church"].

14 Easter Sunday. In the morning 5 went to khristovanie,[72] Papa and Mama gave out eggs. Had breakfast 5 with Papa and Mama on the sofa. Went to Vera's with Anastasia, had tea played in the garden. Went 4 with Papa to the regiment church. Had dinner 4 with Papa and Mama on the sofa.

15 Monday. In the morning 4 went to obednya with Papa at the regiment church. Had breakfast 5 with Papa and Mama on the sofa. In the afternoon we 5 with Papa rode little boats. Had tea with Papa and Mama. Went to Trina's and

---

[68] Ceremonial burial of Christ's shroud on Easter.
[69] Nikolai Pavlovich Sablin's nickname.
[70] Baroness Sophia Karlovna von Buxhoeveden, lady-in-waiting to the empress.
[71] Easter religious services.
[72] Traditional Easter greeting.

played with her Sonia. Had dinner with Anastasia and Mama on the sofa.

16 Tuesday. Went 5 to a grenadier parade. Had breakfast 5 with Aunt Olga and Mama on the sofa. In the afternoon took a walk and rode little boats with Papa and Aunt Olga. Had tea with Mama, Papa and Aunt Olga. Had dinner 4 with Papa and Mama on the sofa. Kiki sent a letter.

17 Wednesday. Went 5 to the parade of the 1st and 2nd sharpshooters regiment. Had breakfast 5. Went to the Invalid House[73] and 4 gave out eggs. Went 4 with Lili to Petersburg. Went to Grandmama's. Then went to Aunt Olga's. We played and had tea and dinner. There were: Sasha and her mother, Irina, Feodor, Count Ungershternberg, Shvedov, Yuzik, Skvortzov, Zborovsky, Klyucharev, Kiki, Kolya, Kulikovksy and Uncle Petya.

18 Thursday. In the morning rode around with Trina and then stopped by the nanny school, there we gave out eggs and played with the children. Had breakfast 5 with Papa and Kostya. In the afternoon took a walk 4 with Papa and rode in little boats. Had tea 4 with Mama and Papa. Had dinner 4 with Papa, Kostya and Mama on the sofa.

---

[73] Sort of a nursing home for the disabled soldiers.

Olga, Maria and Anastasia with an officer and a child. Maria loved little children and wanted to get married and have many.

19 Friday. In the morning we 5 with Papa went to the review of young soldiers. Had breakfast 5 with Papa, Gavril and Mama on the sofa. Went 5 with Papa to the games of the Svodny regiment. Had tea with Mama and Papa. Went 4 to Anya's, Mama and Olga were there and Kleinmichels[74] with [their] mother and Nastenka. Went to Trina's. Had dinner 4 with Gavril and Mama on the sofa.

20 Saturday. In the morning 4 rode around with Trina and stopped by the nanny school. Had breakfast 5 with Papa, Aunt Olga and Mama on the sofa. Went 5 with Papa and

---

[74] Countess Kleinmichel and her two daughters.

Aunt Olga to the games of the Svodny regiment. Had tea 4 with Mama, Papa and Aunt Olga. Went to vsenoshnaya 4 with Papa at the regiment church. Had dinner 4 with Papa and Mama on the sofa.

21 Sunday. Went to obednya with Papa. At breakfast sat with Prince Kochubei and General Asipov. Went to Petersburg. At first went to Grandmama's and then to Aunt Olga's where we played, had tea and dinner. There were: Kanya, Klyucharev, Shangin, Irina and Feodor, Sasha, Nadya, Kolya and their mother, Kulikovsky, Shvedov, Skvortzov, Zborovsky and Uncle Petya.

22 Monday. Had lessons in the morning. Had breakfast 5 with Papa, Ioann and Mama on the sofa. In the afternoon rode bicycles. Had a music lesson. Had tea with Mama and Papa. Went to vsenoshnaya at the regiment church. Had dinner 4 with Papa and Mama on the sofa.

23 Tuesday. In the morning 5 went to church with Papa. Had breakfast 5 with Papa, Mama, Grandmama, Uncle Sandro,[75] Aunt Ksenia, Uncle Petya and Aunt Olga. In the afternoon rode bicycles with Papa and I rode a canoe for the first time. Had tea 4 with Mama and Papa. Had dinner with Anastasia and Alexei.

---

[75] Grand Duke Alexander Mikhailovich, husband of Grand Duchess Ksenia Alexandrovna.

"I rode in a canoe for the first time."

24 Wednesday. Had lessons in the morning. Had breakfast
5 with Papa, Daragan and Mama on the sofa. In the
afternoon rode bicycles with Papa and then in canoes. Had
tea upstairs with Alexei. Had a music lesson. Read with
Trina. Had dinner with Isa and Mama on the sofa.

25 Thursday. In the morning rode with Madame. Then had
lessons. Had breakfast with Papa, Sergei and Mama on the
sofa. In the afternoon rode bicycles with Papa and then in
little boats. Had tea alone. Had music [lesson]. Did
homework and read with Trina. Had dinner with Alexei.

26 Friday. Had lessons in the morning. Had breakfast with Papa, Sashka and Mama on the sofa. In the afternoon rode bicycles with Papa and then in the canoes. Had tea alone. Had music. Anastasia and I had French reading. Did homework. Had dinner with Alexei.

"Rode bicycles with Papa."

27 Saturday. Had lessons in the morning. Had breakfast 5 with Mama on the sofa. In the afternoon took a walk with Papa and rode in canoes. Had tea 4 with Mama and Papa. Went to obednya with Papa to the regiment church for vsenoshnaya. Had dinner with Papa, Sandro and Mama on the sofa.

28 Sunday. In the morning 5 went to obednya at the regiment church with Papa. At breakfast sat with Paparov and Sandro. In the afternoon 4 took a walk with Papa, Anya and Mama in a small carriage. Had tea 4 with Papa and Mama on the balcony, before that rode in canoes. Had dinner with Anastasia and Alexei.

Maria and Olga on the balcony of the Alexander Palace.

29 Monday. Had lessons in the morning. Had breakfast 5 with Papa, Uncle Nikolai[76] and Mama on the sofa. In the afternoon rode bicycles 4 with Papa. Had music. Had tea

---

[76] Grand Duke Nikolai Nikolaevich.

with Mama and Papa. Did homework. Had dinner with Olga, Tatiana, Anya and Mama on the sofa.

With Anastasia and Tatiana in 1913.

30 Tuesday. Had lessons in the morning. Had breakfast 4 with Papa, Aunt Ducky,[77] Uncle Kirill,[78] Uncle Boris and Dmitri. In the afternoon 4 took a walk with Papa and Anya and Mama was in the small carriage. Had tea 4. We 4 had a dance lesson. Had music. Did homework. Had dinner with Anastasia and Alexei.

~

[77] Grand Duchess Viktoria Feodorovna.
[78] Grand Duke Kirill Vladimirovich.

MAY, 1913

1 Wednesday. Had lessons in the morning. Had breakfast we 5 with Papa, Aunt Olga and Mama on the sofa. In the afternoon 4 took a walk with Papa and Aunt Olga. Had tea with Mama, Papa and Aunt Olga. Before that had a music lesson. Did homework. Played with Anastasia and Trina's Sonia. Had dinner with Anastasia and Alexei.

2 Thursday. Had lessons in the morning. Had breakfast 5 with Mama on the sofa. In the afternoon rode around with Tatiana and Nastenka. Had music. Had tea with Mama and Papa. Did homework. Had dinner with Anastasia and Alexei.

3 Friday. Had lessons in the morning. Had breakfast 5 with Papa and Mama on the sofa. In the afternoon rode around with Tatiana and Nastenka. Had music. Had tea with Mama

and Papa. Anastasia and I had French reading. Did homework. Had dinner with Anastasia and Alexei.

4 Saturday. Had lessons in the morning. Ulagov had breakfast with us, I sat with Bobshko and Meshetin. In the afternoon rode around with Tatiana and Nastenka. Had tea 4 with Mama and Papa. 4 went to vsenoshnaya with Papa at the regiment church. Had dinner 4 with Papa, Arsenov, and Mama on the sofa.

5 Sunday. At breakfast sat with Delsal and Dedulin. In the afternoon 4 took a walk with Papa and Aunt Olga, then sledded with Kiki and Papa with Aunt Olga. Had tea 4 with Papa, Mama and Aunt Olga. We 4 sat with Aunt Olga. Had dinner 4 with Papa, Grandmama, Aunt Olga, Uncle Petya, Aunt Ksenia and Uncle Sandro. Then went to hear the Andreev choir and Kiki was there.

6 Monday. 4 with Papa, Grandmama and other relatives went to church and had breakfast there too. I sat with Uncle Sandro and Gavril. In the afternoon rode bicycles and canoes 4 with Papa. Had tea 4 with Papa and Mama. Went to Trina's with Anastasia. Had dinner with Anastasia and Alexei.

7 Tuesday. Rode around with Anastasia and Madame. Had lessons. Went to the regiment church for molebna 5 with Papa. Had breakfast 5 with Papa and Mama on the sofa. In the afternoon took a walk with Papa, then went in boats. Had tea 4. We 4 had dance lessons. Had music. Had dinner

with Anastasia and Alexei. At 11 in the evening Papa left to Berlin for the wedding of the daughter of the German emperor.

"We 4." Maria is on the left.

8 Wednesday. Had lessons in the morning. Had breakfast 5 with Mama on the sofa. Went to nanny school 4 with Nastenka, played with the children in the garden. Had music. Had tea 4 with Mama and Anya. Did homework. Had dinner with Anastasia and Alexei.

9 Thursday. Rode around with Anastasia and Madame. Had lessons. Had breakfast 5 with Aunt Olga and Mama on the sofa. In the afternoon 4 rode around with Aunt Olga then sat on the balcony with Aunt Olga, Mama, Kiki and Anya.

Had tea alone. Anastasia and I had dancing. Had dinner with Anastasia and Alexei.

10 Friday. Had lessons in the morning. Had breakfast 5 with Mama on the sofa. In the afternoon Anastasia and I and Trina went to Vera's and played in the garden. Had music. Had tea with Mama on the balcony. Anastasia and I had French reading. Did homework. Had dinner with Anastasia and Alexei.

Maria posing on a window sill.

11 Saturday. Rode around with Anastasia and Madame. Had lessons. Had breakfast with Anastasia, Alexei and Mama on the sofa. In the afternoon I, Anastasia and Alexei [went] to the nanny school and played with the children in the garden and inside. Had tea 5 with Mama and Irina. 4 went to church of the Svodny regiment. Had dinner 4 with Anya and Mama on the sofa.

12 Sunday. In the morning 5 went to the regiment church. Had breakfast 5 with Mama on the sofa. In the afternoon Anastasia and I and Trina went to Vera's. There we played in the garden and had tea. Went to Trina's. Had dinner with Anastasia and Alexei.

13 Monday. We 5 went to the train station to meet Papa. Had a lesson. Took a walk with Papa. Had lessons. Had breakfast 5 with Papa and Mama on the sofa. In the afternoon 4 with Papa rode our bicycles and in boats. Had music. Had tea with Papa. Went to Trina's. Had dinner 4 with Papa, Grandmama, Aunt Ksenia, Uncle Sandro, Aunt Olga and Uncle Petya.

14 Tuesday. I had food poisoning and didn't go to church. Had breakfast 5 with Papa. In the afternoon sat on the balcony with Mama and Anya. Had tea 4 with Papa. Anastasia and I sat at Trina's. Had dinner with Anastasia and Alexei.

15 Wednesday. Had lessons in the morning. Had breakfast 5 with Papa. In the afternoon took a walk 4 with Papa and

rode in boats. Had tea 4 with Papa and Anya. Went to molebna. Went to the train. At dinner sat with Masalov and Count Benkendorf.

16 Thursday. At breakfast sat with Count Apraksin and Masolov. Went 5 with Papa to Vladimir to the Uspensky Cathedral. From there 4 with Papa on the motors rode to Suzdal. There went to the Suzdal Cathedral then to Spas-Yefimovsky monastery, went to the grave of Prince Pozharsky,[79] from there to Rizolotsky monastery, to Pokrovsky monastery. Had tea in the Igumania's[80] cell. From there went to Bogolubov were in the Cathedral [there]. Papa received the township heads. Had dinner with Anastasia, Alexei, Nilov[81] and Sablin.

---

[79] Prince Dmitry Pozharsky was a Rurik descendant who successfully led the Russian troops against the Poles a year prior to the founding of the Romanov dynasty.
[80] Holy woman and nun.
[81] General-Adjutant Admiral Konstantin Dmitrievich Nilov was the tsar's Flag Captain and one of his friends.

The grand duchesses with extended family at an official function in 1913.

17 Friday. In the morning arrived in [illeg], went 5 with Papa and Mama to the cathedral. There was a litia[82] at the grave of Minin,[83] then went on a Procession of the Cross, to the laying of the foundation of the memorial to Minin and Pozharsky. Had breakfast 5 with Papa and Mama at the palace. In the afternoon we 5 with Papa and Mama had tea at the Nobility meeting. Had dinner with Anastasia, Alexei, Pogulyaev and Sablin.

---

[82] A service held after liturgy or vespers to commemorate departed family members.
[83] Kuzma Minin was a Russian merchant who, along with Prince Pozharsky fought against the Polish invasion.

"We 5 with Papa and Mama."

18 Saturday. In the morning sat on the bridge [of the ship].
At breakfast sat with Botkin and Prince Kochubei. In the
afternoon stayed on the deck. Had tea 5 with Papa and
everyone. At dinner sat with Dedulin and Antonov.

"Stayed on deck... sat with Mama."

19 Sunday. In the morning there was obednya and molebna at the Ipatiev monastery.[84] 5 with Mama and Papa. At breakfast sat with Botkin and Dedulin. In the afternoon we 5 with Papa and Mama saw the Tsar Mikahil Feodorovich's[85] museum. There was tea with the Nobility. Had dinner with Anastasia, Alexei, Nilov and Sablin.

---

[84] Ipatiev monastery in Kostroma was the asylum of the 16-year-old first Romanov tsar and his mother before he was elected.
[85] The first Romanov tsar, elected in 1613

At the Ipatiev Monastery.

20 Monday. In the morning 5 with Mama and Papa to the cathedral. From there went to the laying of the foundation 300 memorial. We 5 with Mama and Aunt Olga went to Bogoyavleisky monastery. At breakfast sat with Dedulin and Botkin. In the afternoon we 4 with Papa went to Resurrection Church in Debryanks. Then looked at the Red Cross hospital, from there went to see the crafts exhibition, where [we] had tea. Had dinner with Anastasia, Alexei, Nilov and Sablin.

21 Tuesday. Arrived in Yaroslavl. We 5 with Papa and Mama went to the Uspensky Cathedral from there 4 with Papa [illeg]...

22 Wednesday. Arrived in Rostov. We 5 with Papa went to the Uspensky Cathedral, then walked along Kra[illeg] from there to the White Chamber and Princely Tower. On the way looked at churches. At breakfast sat with Count Benkendorf and Mosolov. In the afternoon we went to the Pokrovsky monastery and church of St Ioann. Had tea 5 with Papa and the suite. Went to vsenoshnaya at the Christ's Resurrection church. At dinner sat with Benkendorf and Mosolov.

"Mama" and OTMA sharing a meal with the suite.

23 Thursday. Arrived in Petrovsk with Papa. Went to obednya at the city cathedral. At breakfast sat with Alexei and Trotsky. Drove to Pereslav in motors. Went to Nikitsky monastery where we were blessed by [illeg]. Then went to Danilovsky monastery and also in Feodorovsky [illeg] monastery.

24 Friday. We 4 with Papa went to obednya at the Sergeyev Lavra and had tea with Metropolit.[86] At breakfast sat with Benkendorf and Bulygin. Went to Moscow, from the [train] station we went to the Kremlin to the [illeg]. Had tea 4 with Papa, Mama, Aunt Olga and Aunt Ksenia. Had dinner 4 with Papa and Aunt Ella.

25 Saturday. There was a [Ceremonial] Exit from the Red Porch and I was walking arm in arm with Uncle Sandro. There was an obednya at the Uspensky Cathedral [illeg] picked up gold coins. At breakfast sat with Uncle Sandro and Uncle Alek [?]. In the afternoon we 4 with Papa looked at [illeg] then went to the bridge of imprisonment of St Hermogen and looked at the house of the Boyars Romanovs.[87] Had tea 4 with Papa, Dmitri and Marie[88]. Had dinner with Anastasia and Alexei.

---

[86] Metropolitan Bishop in Orthodox Church.
[87] Boyars Romanovs were wealthy noble family, who produced the first Romanov tsar. Their mansion on Varvarka Street in Moscow still exists and is a museum today.
[88] Grand Duke Dmitri Pavlovich and Grand Duchess Maria Pavlovna, first cousins of the tsar.

At the house of Boyars Romanov in Moscow.

26 Sunday. In the morning 5 with Papa went to obednya at the NovoSpassky monastery and there was litia at the grave. Had breakfast 5 with Papa, Aunt Olga at Aunt Ella's.   In the afternoon 4 and Papa with her went to the school of the middle merchant society, had tea there. Had dinner 4 with Papa.

27 Monday. In the morning 4 with Papa saw an exhibit at the Stroganoff School. Had breakfast 5 with Mama on the sofa, Aunt Ella and Marie. In the afternoon we 5 with Papa,

Mama and Aunt Ella went to the Voznesensky Monastery. From there went to the train. Had tea 4 with Papa and the suite. At dinner sat with Count Benkendorf and Veselkovsky.

Maria riding in a carriage with "Aunt Ella" and her sisters during the tercentenary celebrations.

28 Tuesday. In the morning arrived at T.S. We 5 with Papa went to molebna at the lower regiment church. Had breakfast 5 with Papa, Veselkin and Mama on the sofa. In the afternoon rode around with Trina. Had tea 4 with Papa and Mama. Had dinner 4 with Papa, Veselkin and Mama on the sofa.

29 Wednesday. In the morning we had moleben. Had breakfast 5 with Papa, Aunt Olga, Aunt Ksenia, Uncle Sandro and the children. In the afternoon I stayed home and read

with Trina. Had tea with Mama, Papa and Irina. Had dinner with Anastasia, Alexei and 4 little Ai Todortzy.

30 Thursday. I have fever, in the morning was 38.7 and sore throat and headache. They transferred me to Tatiana's room, I stayed in bed and Shura[89] read to me. Had breakfast in bed. Temp. 38.8. Then Shura again read to me. Had tea. Temp. 38.4. Had dinner. Temp 38.1. [Crossed out] and Papa before dinner.

31 Friday. In the morning temp 36.9. Read with Trina. Had breakfast. Temp. 37. Read with Trina and played cards with Trina [illeg] and Liza. Sonia was here, Mama was here and Anya. Temp. 36.3. Read with Trina. Had dinner. [illeg] was here. Temp 37.7.

~

---

[89] Alexandra Alexandrovna Tegleva, nurse to Grand Duchess Anastasia and eventual wife of Pierre Gilliard.

JUNE, 1913

1 Saturday. Dark in the morning, got up from bed and got dressed. Had breakfast with Anastasia, played cards with Alexei. Had tea in bed. [illeg] at Mama's and Papa's. Had dinner with Alexei.   Temp at 6 o'cl. 37. After dinner at 9 o'cl. 36.9

2 Sunday. 5 went with Papa to a parade of the Izmailovsky Regiment and Northern Battalion. Had breakfast 5 with Aunt Mavra[90] and Mama on the sofa. In the afternoon 4 went in a motor with Anya to Aunt Olga's in Peterhof. Had tea, took a walk. Played and had dinner. There were: Shvedov, Yuzik, Skvortzov, Zborovsky, Rodionov, Klyucharev, Kulikovsky, Aunt Ksenia with Irina, Andrusha and Feodor and Anya and Semyonov. Returned home.

---

[90] Grand Duchess Elizaveta Mavrikievna, wife of Grand Duke Konstantin Konstantinovich.

3 Monday. Went 4 to obednya. Had breakfast 5 with Papa and Mama on the sofa. In the afternoon Anastasia and I with Trina went to Vera's and Georgiy's[91] where we played in the garden and had tea. Went to Trina's. Had dinner with Anastasia and Alexei.

Maria and Anastasia with an officer in 1913.

4 Tuesday. In the morning went with Agatha Evgenievna to the nanny school. Had breakfast 5 with Papa, Bagration and Mama on the sofa. In the afternoon drove from T.S. to Peterhof. Had tea 5 with Mama and Papa. Had dinner 4 with Papa, Aunt Olga and Mama on the sofa.

---

[91] Princess Vera Konstantinovna and Prince Georgiy Konstantinovich, youngest children of Grand Duke Konstantin Konstantinovich.

The Nanny School of Tsarskoe Selo, as it looked when Maria visited there.

5 Wednesday. 4 went to molebna with Mama. Had breakfast 5 with Mama, Papa, Ioannchik with Uncle Niki.[92] In the afternoon took a walk with Papa. Had tea with Papa, Mama, Aunt Olga and Sonia Dehn and her boy. Had dinner with Anastasia and Alexei.

6 Thursday. The dentist was here in the morning. Had breakfast 5 Papa, Mama, Aunt Ksenia, Uncle Sandro and their children. Went to Aunt Olga's had tea there and played. [There] were: Shvedov, Yuzik, Skvortzov, Zborovsky,

---

[92] Grand Duke Nicholas Konstaninovich.

Kulikovsky and Aunt Ksenia with 4 strannitzy.[93] Had dinner with Anastasia and Alexei.

7 Friday. In the morning 4 went to Tatiana's in Strelna and saw Teymuraz.[94] Went to Countess Hendrikova.[95] Had breakfast 5 with Papa, Mama, Aunt Olga, Uncle Niki and Dmitri. In the afternoon took a walk with Papa. Had tea 4 with Mama and Papa. Had dinner with Mama.

8 Saturday. In the morning rode around with Trina. Had breakfast 5 with Papa, Mama, Dmitri and [illeg] Monaksky[?]. In the afternoon 4 went to Anya's, there were Anya's parents, Purtzeladze, Eristov and Ravtopulo.[96] Had tea 4 with Mama and Papa. Went 4 to vsenoshnaya. Had dinner 4 with Papa and Mama on the sofa.

9 Sunday. Went 4 with Papa to a parade of the Equestrian Grenadier Regiment. Had breakfast 4 with Count Apraksin and Olga Evgenievna[97] and Mama on the sofa. In the afternoon we with Papa, Mama and Aunt Olga [went] to the "Alexandria"[98] where we had tea. Arrived in Kronshtadt and went to the "Standart."[99] At dinner sat with Zelenetzky and Sablin.

---

[93] Holy women.
[94] Prince Teymuraz Bagration-Mukhransky, son of Princess Tatiana Konstantinovna.
[95] Mother of "Nastenka" Hendrikova.
[96] Officer Boris Ravtopulo
[97] Lady in waiting Olga Evgenievna Butsova.
[98] One of the Imperial yachts.
[99] The main Imperial yacht.

On the "Standart."

10 Monday.   In the morning we 4 went to the consecration of the Navy Cathedral in Kronshtadt with Papa. At breakfast sat with Nilov and Babitzyn. In the afternoon was on the deck and in the cabin. Had tea 4 with Papa, the ladies and officers. Sat with Pi and Nastenka. Had dinner with Mama.

Maria reading on the deck of the "Standart."

11 Tuesday. In the morning 4 with Nastenka and Trina went to [illeg] and Aunt Olga. At breakfast sat with Sangovich and Polushkin. In the afternoon took a walk on the "patio" with Papa, Aunt Olga, the ladies and officers. Had tea with Loya. Had dinner with Mama.

12 Wednesday. In the morning 4 with Nastenka, Trina and M.K. went to the mater[?] and Aunt Olga was there. At breakfast sat with Zelenetzky and Myasoyedov Ivanov. In the afternoon sat with Mama and Kiki. Had tea 4 with Papa, Aunt Olga and officers and ladies. Had dinner with Mama and [...]

13 Thursday. In the morning went to the Lily of Valley island with Trina, Nastenka and L.A.B. and Aunt Olga was there. At breakfast sat with Zelenetzky and Kuzminsky. In the afternoon took a walk on "patio" with Papa, Aunt Olga, the ladies and officers. Had tea 4 with them. At dinner sat with Schetatveli and Anurkov. In the evening played with Anya, Nastenka, Pi, L.M., K.A. N. and Arsenoev.

14 Friday. In the morning we 5 with Papa and Aunt Olga went to moleben. At breakfast sat with [illeg] and Nilov. In the afternoon went ashore with Papa, Aunt Olga, the ladies and officers, played tennis, I with Anastasia and Aunt Olga ran around barefoot. Had tea 4 with [illeg]. At dinner sat with Papa and Nilov. In the evening sat 4 with Pi, Kolya and Nastenka. Rose from a bouquet from Yalta.

On the tennis court in 1913.

15 Saturday. In the morning stayed on the yacht. At breakfast sat with Nilov and Saltanov. In the afternoon went ashore played tennis and swung on giant steps.[100] Had tea 4 with [illeg]. Read with Trina. At dinner sat with Babitzyn and Rodionov. In the evening talked with Pi and Nastenka.

16 Sunday. In the morning 5 with Papa went to obednya on the deck. At breakfast sat with Nilov and Sangovich. In the afternoon sat with Mama and Kiki on the yacht. Had tea 4 with Papa, Aunt Olga, the ladies and officers. Had dinner with Anastasia and Alexei.

17 Monday. In the morning stayed on the yacht. At breakfast sat with Papa and Nilov. In the afternoon went ashore played tennis with baiblo popi [?] and swung on giant steps with Papa, Aunt Olga, the ladies and officers. Had tea 4 with the same. Read with Trina. Had dinner with Mama.

---

[100] A swing-like game.

"...swung on giant steps."

18 Tuesday. In the morning stayed on the yacht. At breakfast sat with Zelenetzky and Shvedov. In the afternoon went ashore swung on giant steps and played tennis with S. V. Z., Nastenka and Arsenoev. Had tea 4 with Papa, Aunt Olga on the "Polar Star." In the cabin compania sat with Nalb[illeg] and played on the [illeg]. Had dinner with Anastasia and Alexei.

19 Wednesday. In the morning stayed on the yacht. At breakfast sat with Kiki and [blank]. In the afternoon went ashore, played tennis with L.M.K., Anastasia and Tatiana then with Arsenoev with Nastenka and Anastasia. Had tea 4 with Papa, ladies and officers who were on the shore. Played [illeg] I with Anastasia and Tatiana and Olga with Pi and Nastenka. At dinner sat with Kiki and [illeg].

20 Thursday. In the morning stayed on the yacht. At breakfast sat with Nilov and in the afternoon went ashore, played tennis I with Zelenetzky, Anastasia and Arsenoev. Had tea 4 with Papa, Aunt Olga, ladies and officers who were on the shore. Read with Anastasia and Trina. Had dinner with Mama.

Maria and Anastasia with their rackets "...played tennis."

21 Friday. In the morning I rode in a dvoika[101] with Papa and Anastasia. At breakfast sat with Papa and Zelenetzky. In the afternoon sat on the deck with Mama and Kiki. Had

---

[101] Carriage drawn by a pair of horses, as opposed to "troika" with three horses.

tea 4 with Papa, Aunt Olga, ladies and officers. Read with Anastasia and Trina. Had dinner with Mama.

Maria, Anastasia, and Olga posing with officers.

22 Saturday. In the morning stayed on the yacht. At breakfast sat with Zelenetzky and Saltanov. In the afternoon went ashore, played tennis and swung on giant steps. Had tea 4 with Papa, Aunt Olga, officers and ladies. Went to vsenohsnaya on deck 4 with Papa. At dinner sat with Nilov and Zelenetzky. Talked at first with Kolya, then with Pi.

23 Sunday. In the morning 4 with Papa went to obednya on deck. At breakfast sat with Papa and Prince Vyazemsky. In the afternoon went ashore played tennis with Arseneov, and L.A.V. Had tea 4 with Papa, Aunt Olga, ladies and officers. Went 4 with Papa, Aunt Olga, ladies and officers from the yacht on [illeg] and team on "patio." At first there was a show, the sailors performed. Then dancing, then supper, I sat with Pi. Then there was a [illeg] and dancing again, after which we left which was 12 o'cl.

The grand duchesses dancing with officers on the "Standart."

24 Monday. In the morning was lying in bed. At breakfast sat with Gavrilov. In the afternoon sat with Mama and Kiki on the deck. Had tea 4 with Papa, Aunt Olga, ladies and officers. Read with Trina. Had dinner with Mama.

25 Tuesday. In the morning stayed on the yacht. At breakfast sat with Zheno and Kubero. In the afternoon went ashore played tennis. Had tea 4 with Papa, Aunt Olga,

ladies and officers who were on the shore. At dinner sat with Zelenetzky and Zlebov. There was a cinematograph in the dining room, they showed houses of Dolgorukys[102] and [illeg].

26 Wednesday. In the morning stayed on the yacht. At breakfast sat with Zelenetzky and Kiki. In the afternoon went ashore and played tennis with Papa, Aunt Olga, ladies and officers. Had tea with the same. Had dinner with Mama.

Maria "...on the yacht."

---

[102] The Dolgorukys are an old Russian noble family descended from the Ruriks

27 Wednesday. In the morning stayed on the yacht. At breakfast sat with Nilov and Kiki. In the afternoon went ashore played tennis, Papa, Aunt Olga, ladies and officers. Had tea with the same. Read with Trina, had dinner with Mama.

28 Friday. In the morning stayed on the yacht. Aunt Olga left for the "Polar Star." At breakfast sat with Nilov and Kiki. In the afternoon stayed on the yacht with Mama. Sat on the deck with Kiki and Mama but at first with Kolya. Had tea with Papa, ladies and officers who were on the shore. Read with Trina. Had dinner with Mama.

Maria with an officer.

29 Saturday. In the morning stayed on the yacht. At breakfast sat with Zlebov and Nilov. In the afternoon went

to tennis, I played with Nastenka with K[illeg] and Zlebov. Went 4 to vsenoshnaya on deck with Papa. At dinner sat with Papa and Nilov. Talked with Kiki and Kolya. [Got] a rose from Yerivantzy from their parade.

Maria and her sisters "on deck" of the yacht "The Standart."

30 Sunday. In the morning 4 with Papa went to obednya on deck. At breakfast sat with Prince Vyazemsky and [blank]. In the afternoon went to tennis, I with Drenteln, Anastasia and Nastenka. Had tea with Papa, officers and ladies who were on shore. Had dinner with Papa. Before dinner read with Trina.

~

JULY, 1913

1 Monday. In the morning [we] stayed on the yacht. At breakfast sat with Papa and Nilov. In the afternoon went to shore and played tennis with Drenteln, Anastasia and [illeg]. Had tea with the ladies and officers who were at the shore.

2 Tuesday. In the morning went swimming with Tatiana and Shura. At breakfast sat with Papa and Kerber. In the afternoon stayed with Mama and Kiki on the deck. Had tea 4 with Papa, the ladies and officers who were on the shore. Read with Trina. Had dinner with Mama.

3 Wednesday. In the morning went swimming with Tatiana and Shura. At breakfast sat with Zelenkin and Vysotsky. Went to tennis, I played with Papa, Tatiana and Pi. Had tea 4 with those who were at the shore. At dinner sat with

Papa and Butakov.[103] Departed to Revel with Raid Standart at 3 o'cl.

Maria's smile

4 Thursday. There was a fog. Arrived in Revel, Papa went to the "Rurik" for the shooting.[104] At breakfast sat with Grigorovich and Essen. Had tea 4 with Papa and the ladies. Went to Raid Standart at 3 o'cl. At dinner sat with Kiki and Kublitsky.

---

[103] Husband of Olga Evgenievna
[104] Presumably shooting exercises.

5 Friday. In the morning swam with Tatiana and Shura. At breakfast sat with Papa and Zelenetsky. In the afternoon went to tennis, I played S.T.,[105] Anastasia and Nastenka. Had tea 4 with Papa, the ladies and officers who were at the shore. Talked 4 with Kolya, Mimka and S.T. Read with Trina. Had dinner with Mama.

6 Saturday. In the morning swam with Tatiana and Shura. At breakfast sat with Papa and Shilov. In the afternoon went ashore, played with Anastasia, Nastenka and Ippolit. Had tea 4 with Papa, the ladies and officers who were at the shore. Went 4 with Papa to vsenoshnaya on the deck. At dinner sat with Nilov and Zelenetzky. Played cards with Nastenka, Count Grabbe, Kotebinsky and Pi.

---

[105] The maid of Grand Duchess Olga Alexandrovna ("Aunt Olga").

Maria and Olga with an officer on the "Standart."

7 Sunday. In the morning 4 went to obednya on deck with Papa. At breakfast sat with Papa and Prince Vyazemsky. In the afternoon went ashore, played tennis. Had tea 4 with Papa, the ladies and officers who were at the shore. Read with Trina. Had dinner with Mama.

8 Monday. In the morning swam with Tatiana, Anya and Shura. At breakfast sat with Nilov and Kiki. In the afternoon sat with Mama and Kiki on deck. Went to navigator's cabin. Had tea 4 with Papa, the ladies and officers who were at the shore. Had dinner with Mama. Before dinner read with Trina.

With officers on deck in 1913.

9 Tuesday. In the morning 4 with Papa watched "Kazanetz" and then went out to sea on "[illeg]", rocked [the ship]. Had breakfast with Mama and Alexei. In the afternoon went ashore. Had tea with Papa, the ladies and officers who were at the shore. Read with Trina. Had dinner with Mama.

10 Wednesday. Rode with Anya and Shura. At breakfast sat with Papa and Nilov. In the afternoon sat on deck with Mama and Kiki. Had tea 4 with the ladies and officers who were at the shore. At dinner sat with Schepochka[106] and

---

[106] Presumably the nickname of one of the officers, literally means a small piece of wood in Russian

Kiki. We 4 with Mama and Papa went to the navigator's cabin and played bingo, it was really nice.

"We 4."

11 Thursday. In the morning swam with Tatiana and Anya. Went to molebna on deck 4 with Papa. At breakfast sat with Zelenetzky and Prince Vyazemsky. In the afternoon went to tennis, played with S.T.SH., Nastenka and Anastasia. Had tea with Mama. Went to navigator's cabin with Kiki. At dinner sat with Papa and Zelenetzky. Talked with [illeg], Kolya and Ippolit.

12 Friday. In the morning left from Raid Standart to Kronshtadt. At breakfast sat with Papa and Nilov. In the afternoon talked with Ippolit, Pi and Kolya. Left the yacht to the "Alexandria" and [headed] to Peterhof. It was very

boring and sad. Had tea 5 with Mama and Papa. Ran around the garden. Had dinner with Anastasia and Alexei.

Maria at Peterhof in 1913.

13 Saturday. In the morning went to the garden. Had breakfast 5 with Papa and Count Fredericks. In the afternoon played tennis, we 4 with Papa and Nastenka. Had tea 4 with Mama and Papa. Went 4 to vsenoshnaya. Had dinner 4 with Papa and Mama on the sofa.

14 Sunday. In the morning went to obednya with Papa. At breakfast sat with Count Rostovtzev and [illeg]. In the afternoon 4 played tennis with Papa, Anya and Kolya. Had tea 4 with Mama and Papa. Ran around the garden. Had dinner with Anastasia and Alexei.

15 Monday. In the morning watched a film. The yacht was leaving for Crimea. Had a Russian lesson. Had breakfast 5 with Papa and Mama on the sofa. In the afternoon played tennis 4 with Papa and Anya. Had tea 4 with Papa and Mama. Read with Trina. Had dinner with Anastasia and Alexei.

16 Tuesday. In the morning had a Russian and music lessons. Had breakfast 5 with Papa and Mama on the sofa. In the afternoon 4 played tennis with Papa, Nastenka, S.T.SH. and Poupse.[107] Had tea 4 with Papa and Mama. Read with Trina. Had dinner with Anastasia.

17 Wednesday. In the morning had Russian and music lessons. Had breakfast 4 with Papa and Dehn. In the afternoon played tennis 4 with Papa, Nastenka and Anya. Had tea 4 with Papa. Had dinner with Anastasia.

18 Thursday. In the morning had a Russian and music lessons. Had breakfast 4 with Papa, Aunt Ella and Uncle Nikolai. In the afternoon played tennis with Papa, Anya,

---

[107] Presumably a nickname of one of the suite or officers; it literally means "baby doll."

Mishka and S.T.SH. Had tea 4 with Papa, Mama and Aunt Ella. Anastasia and I went to vsenoshnaya in [illeg] with Aunt Ella. Had dinner with Anastasia.

19 Friday. Had music and Russian language lessons in the morning. At breakfast sat with Papa and Aunt Ella. In the afternoon played tennis with Papa and Anya. Had tea 4 with Mama, Papa and Aunt Ella. Had dinner with Anastasia.

20 Saturday. In the morning had a Russian language lesson. Had breakfast 4 with Aunt Ella. In the afternoon played with Papa and Anya. Went to vsenoshnaya 4 with Aunt Ella. Had dinner 4 with Papa and Aunt Ella.

21 Sunday. In the morning 4 went to obednya with Papa and Aunt Ella. Had breakfast with Papa, Aunt Ella and Aunt Irene.[108] In the afternoon took a walk with Papa and rode in boats. Had tea 4 with Papa, Mama, Aunt Ella and Aunt Irene. Had dinner 4 with Papa, Aunt Ella and Aunt Irene.

---

[108] Princess Irene of Prussia, sister of the Empress.

Maria picking flowers.

22 Monday. In the morning went to obednya 4 with Papa.
At breakfast sat with Dedulin and empty [seat]. In the
afternoon 4 played tennis with Papa, Anya, Mishka and
S.T.SH. Had tea 4 with Papa, Mama, Aunt Ella and Aunt
Irene. Had dinner with Papa, Aunt Ella and Aunt Irene. In
the evening took a walk in Peterhof with Papa.

23 Tuesday. In the morning had music lesson. Had
breakfast 4 with Papa, Aunt Irene and Uncle Andrei.[109] In
the afternoon colored [illeg] 5 with Mama and Aunt Irene.

---

[109] Grand Duke Andrei Vladimirovich.

Had tea 4 with Mama and Aunt Irene. Had dinner with Aunt Irene and Mama on the sofa.

24 Wednesday. In the morning rode with Aunt Irene, then had music [lesson]. Had breakfast we 3 little ones with Aunt Irene and Mama on the sofa. In the afternoon 4 played tennis with Papa, Anya, Mishka and the Baron. Had tea 4 with Papa, Mama and Aunt Irene. Had dinner with Dmitri, Aunt Irene and Mama on the sofa.

25 Thursday. Had music in the morning. Had breakfast we 3 little ones with Anya and Mama on the sofa. In the afternoon 4 with Mama. Had tea 4 with Mama and Aunt Irene. Read with Trina. Had dinner with Anastasia and Alexei.

26 Friday. In the morning had music and Russian language. Had breakfast 4 with Papa and Aunt Irene. In the afternoon 4 played tennis. Had tea 4 with Mama and Aunt Irene. Read with Trina. Had dinner with Anastasia and Alexei.

27 Saturday. In the morning had Russian lesson. Had breakfast 5 with Aunt Irene and Mama on the sofa. In the afternoon 4 played tennis with Anya. Had tea 4 with Papa, Mama and Aunt Irene. Went 4 to vsenoshnaya. Had dinner 4 with Aunt Irene and Mama on the sofa. In the evening [we] played cards.

28 Sunday. In the morning 4 went to obednya with Papa.
Had breakfast 4 with Papa and Aunt Irene. In the afternoon
played tennis 4 with Papa, Anya, Mishka and the Baron.
Had tea 4 with Papa, Mama and Aunt Irene. 4 with Aunt
Irene went to the Babbigons. Had dinner with Anastasia
and Alexei.

29 Monday. In the morning 4 went horseback riding. Had
God's Law and Russian language lessons. Had breakfast 5
with Mama on the sofa. In the afternoon played tennis
with Nastenka. Had tea 4 with Mama and Aunt Irene. Read
with Trina. Had dinned 4 with Aunt Irene and Mama on the
sofa. In the evening played cards.

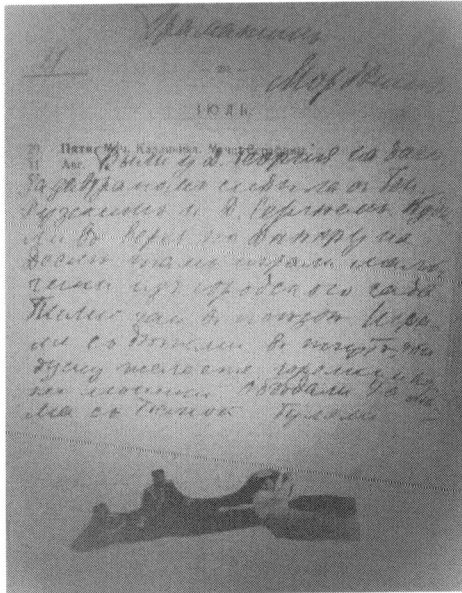

Page from Maria's 1913 diary for 29 July, where she cut out and
pasted a photo she took.

30 Tuesday. In the morning 4 went to obednya with Papa and Aunt Irene. At breakfast sat with Nilov and empty space. In the afternoon sat with Mama and Aunt Irene. Had tea 4 with Mama, Papa, Aunt Irene. Anastasia and I went to Aunt Irene's farm. Had dinner with Anastasia and Alexei.

31 Wednesday. In the morning took walk with Aunt Irene and Lori. Had breakfast 3 little ones with Aunt Irene and Mama on the sofa. In the afternoon drove to Krasnoe Selo with Aunt Irene and Lori. There was a review of the 8th Voznesensky Uhlan [regiment] and 3rd Elizavetgradsky Hussar regiment. Returned with Aunt Irene and Lori. Had dinner with Aunt Irene and Mama on the sofa.

~

AUGUST, 1913

1 Thursday. In the morning read with Trina. Had breakfast
4 with Papa and Aunt Irene. In the afternoon 4 with Papa
and Aunt Irene went to the [illeg] factory. Had tea with
Mama, Papa and Aunt Irene. Anastasia and I went to Aunt
Irene's. Had dinner with Anastasia.

"...with Anastasia..." in 1913.

2 Friday. In the morning had music and God's Law lessons. Had breakfast with Aunt Irene and Mama on the sofa. In the afternoon 4 played tennis with Papa, Anya and Mishka. Had tea 4 with Mama, Papa and Aunt Irene. Went to Orenianbaum with Aunt Irene. Had dinner with Anastasia and Alexei.

3 Saturday. Had music and God's Law lessons. Had breakfast 4 with Papa, Aunt Miechen, Aunt Ducky, Aunt Irene and Uncle Kirill. In the afternoon 4 went with Papa and Aunt Irene to see the maneuvers at Krasnoe [Selo]. Had tea with Aunt Irene there. Returned home 4 with Aunt Irene. Had dinner 4 with Aunt Irene and Mama on the sofa. Played cards.

4 Sunday. In the morning 4 went to obednya. Had breakfast 5 with Aunt Irene and Mama on the sofa. In the afternoon 4 played tennis with Nastenka and Lori. Went to Aunt Mops's with Aunt Irene. Had tea 4 with Mama and Aunt Irene. Rode around 4 with Aunt Irene. Had dinner with Anastasia and Alexei.

5 Monday. In the morning went to the review of the 3rd Elizavetgradsky Hussar regiment and the 8th Voznesensky Uhlan [regiment]. Olga and Tatiana did racing. Had breakfast with Aunt Irene and Mama. In the afternoon 4 with Papa and Dmitri walked around our garden with walking sticks. Had tea 4 with Mama, Papa, Aunt Irene and Dmitri. Went 4 to vsenoshnaya. Had dinner 4 with Aunt

Irene and Mama on the sofa. Saw Aunt Irene off to [illeg. smeared ink].

"Walked... with our walking sticks."

6 Tuesday. 4 went to obednya. Had breakfast 5 with Nastenka and Mama on the sofa. In the afternoon 5 with Papa and Uncle Kirill went to the "Alexandria" and the "Rabotnik."[110] Had tea 4 with Mama and Papa. Read with Trina. Had dinner 4 with Mama on the sofa. [written in pencil:] I had a headache and temperature was 38.6.

---

[110] "The Worker"

7 Wednesday. I have temp. 39.3. Went to the train. Was lying down in bed. Temp. 39.7. Drank broth. Shura read to me. Very bad stomach ache. Temp.... [entry ends]

Maria ill in bed with her sisters and parents.

21 August- 22 September - no entries [presumably due to Maria's illness]

10 Saturday. In the morning was lying down on the sofa. Had breakfast in bed, Mama on the sofa.

11 Sunday. In the morning was lying down on the sofa at Mama's. Had breakfast with Mama [crossed out]. Stayed

on [illeg] sat with Mama and Kiki and had tea with them. Sat with Babitzyn and Kozhevnikov. Had dinner with Anastasia and Mama on the sofa.

12 Monday. In the morning stayed on the yacht. Had breakfast with Mama. In the afternoon stayed on the yacht, sat with Mama and Kiki, had tea with them. Sat with Pi and Kolya. Had dinner with Anastasia and Mama on the sofa.

13 Tuesday. In the morning stayed on the yacht. Had breakfast with Mama. In the afternoon Shkermansky and Balaklavsky battle fields. Had tea with Papa and Aunt Olga. Sat with Pi and Kolya. At dinner sat with Nilov and Dedulin. Sat with Pi, Kolya Zlebov, Stanitza, Mordvinov[111] and Aunt Olga.

14 Wednesday. In the morning departed Sevastopol to Yalta. At breakfast sat with Grinvaldom and Prince Trubetzkoy. Arrived in Yalta, went to our house. There was a moleben. Had tea 4 with Papa, Mama and Aunt Olga. Went to vsenoshnaya. Had dinner 4 with Papa, Aunt Olga and Mama on the sofa.

15 Thursday. In the morning went to obednya with Papa and Aunt Olga. At breakfast sat with Komarov and Dedulin. In the afternoon took a walk with Papa and Aunt Olga. Had tea 4 with Mama, Papa and Aunt Olga. Had dinner with Anastasia and Alexei.

---

[111] Fligel Adjutant,Colonel A.A. *Mordvinov*

16 Friday. In the morning took a walk with Papa, Aunt Olga, Anya, Drenteln and Mordvinov to Kharax.[112] Then went swimming with Papa and Aunt Olga. At breakfast sat with Dedulin and Apraksin. In the afternoon went to Ai Danil 4 with Papa, Aunt Olga, Prince Gagarin and the suite. Took a walk there. Had tea 4 with Papa, Mama and Aunt Olga. Had dinner with Anastasia.

17 Saturday. In the morning swam with Papa and Aunt Olga. Went to molebna at the "Standart" 5 with Papa and Aunt Olga. At breakfast sat with Nilov and Zlebov. Then [we] danced, it was very merry. Had tea 4 with Mama, Papa and Aunt Olga. Went 4 to vsenoshnaya. At dinner sat with Prince Trubetzkoy and Iyurikovsky.

---

[112] An English-style palace in the Crimea, home to Grand Duke Georgiy Mikhailovich. It was named after the largest Roman military settlement excavated in the region.

Maria and her family on the "Standart."

18 Sunday. In the morning went to obednya with Papa and
Aunt Olga. At breakfast sat with Nilov and Dumbadze.[113] In
the afternoon 4 took a walk with Papa and Aunt Olga and
them went swimming. Had tea 4 with Mama, Papa and
Aunt Olga. Sat with Aunt Olga. Had dinner with Anastasia
and Alexei.

---

[113] Ivan Antonovich Dumbadze, Major-General of the Tsar's
Retinue.

Maria and "Aunt Olga."

19 Monday. In the morning went swimming with Papa and Aunt Olga. At breakfast sat with Dedulin and Mordvinov. In the afternoon 4 took a walk to Oreanda[114] with Papa and Aunt Olga. Had tea 4 with Mama, Papa and Aunt Olga. Had dinner with Anastasia and Alexei.

20 Tuesday. In the morning 4 with Papa and Aunt Olga took a walk and went swimming. At breakfast sat with Drenteln and Dedulin. In the afternoon took a drive with Papa, Aunt Olga and the suite to Aitetri and Eagle's Landing. Had tea 4 with Papa, Mama and Aunt Olga. Had dinner with Anastasia and Alexei.

---

[114] Ruins of the Oreanda Palace, which was built for Empress Alexandra Feodorovna (wife of Tsar Nicholas I). It was lost in a fire in 1882.

21 Wednesday. In the morning took a walk and went swimming with Papa and Aunt Olga. At breakfast sat with Komarov and Nikitin. In the afternoon 4 with Papa, Aunt Olga and the suite [went] to a farm. Had tea 4 with Papa, Mama, Aunt Olga, Anya and Kiki. Sat with Aunt Olga. Had dinner with Anastasia and Alexei.

Maria at Livadia.

22 Thursday. Blank.

23 Friday. In the morning went to Yalta with Anastasia and Aunt Olga. Had breakfast with Mama. In the afternoon sat with Mama on the balcony. Had tea 4 with Mama, Papa and Aunt Olga. With Aunt Olga took a ride to the Apraksins. Had dinner with Anastasia and Alexei. Had an ear-ache, temp. 38.1.

24 Saturday. In the morning temp 37, stayed in bed. Had breakfast there too. In the afternoon sat [crossed off] was lying down with Mama. Temp. 36.7. Had tea alone, sat with Aunt Olga. Temp. 37.3. Had dinner alone.

25 Sunday. In the morning was lying down on the sofa. Had breakfast alone. In the afternoon sat at Mama's and was lying down on the sofa. Had tea alone. Played cards with Shura. Had dinner alone.

26 Monday. In the morning was lying down in bed. Had breakfast with Mama. Was lying down, Mama, Kiki and Anya came to see me. Had tea alone. Played cards with Liza[115] and Shura. Had dinner alone. In the morning temp. 36.9. In the afternoon 36.3. Evening 37.1.

27 Tuesday. In the morning stayed in bed. Had breakfast with Mama and Alexei. Trina, Shura and Liza sat with me. Had tea alone. Played cards. Had dinner alone. In the morning temp. 36.3 afternoon 36.9, evening 36.5.

---

[115] The grand duchesses' maid

28 Wednesday. In the morning stayed in bed. Had breakfast with Mama. In the afternoon sat [crossed out] was lying down. Shura and Trina read. Had tea alone. Had dinner alone. In the morning temp. 36.3, afternoon 36.6, evening 37.1.

29 Thursday. In the morning stayed in bed. Had breakfast with Mama and Alexei. In the afternoon was lying down, Shura and Trina read. Had tea alone. Had dinner alone. In the morning temp. 36.6, afternoon 36.4, evening 37.

30 Friday. Got up on the morning. Went to [illeg] for obednya. Had breakfast with Mama on the sofa. In the afternoon went to tennis 4 with Papa, Mama and Aunt Olga, Anya, Zelenetzky, Kiki, Kolya and Pi were there. Had tea at tennis [court]. Had dinner 4 with Papa, Aunt Olga, Mordvinov and Mama on the sofa. In the morning 36.3, evening 36.8

31 Saturday. In the morning walked to the beach. Had breakfast with Mama on the sofa. In the afternoon took a walk with Anya. Had tea with Mama, Kiki and Anya. Went to vsenoshnaya at the [illeg]. Had dinner 4 with Papa and Mama on the sofa. In the morning 36.5, evening 36.5.

~

SEPTEMBER, 1913

1 Sunday. In the morning 4 with Papa went to obednya. Sat with Gr. A praising and Nilov. In the afternoon 4 with Mama and Papa went to tennis, Anna, Pi, Kolya and Georg. Makov. Had tea in the little house. Had dinner with Anastasia and Alexei.

2 Monday. In the morning walked right with Papa to the beach house. At breakfast sat with Sukhomlinov. Two officers from my regiment were there. In the afternoon played tennis 4 with Papa, Anya, Kiki, Kolya, Pi and Petrovsky. Had tea with them at home. Went to Irina's and played with [...] grandson. Had dinner with Anastasia and Alexei.

With "...officers from my regiment."

3 Tuesday. I'm the morning walked to the beach with Papa. At breakfast sat with Nilov and Drenteln. In the afternoon played tennis 4 with Papa, Mama, Anya, Kiki, Kolya and Petrovsky were there. Had tea during tennis. Played with grandchildren at Trina's and read in French. Had dinner with Anastasia and Vyazemsky.

4 Wednesday. Had lessons in the morning, walked to the beach. At breakfast sat with Smirnov and Dedulin. In the afternoon played tennis 4 with Papa, Mama, Anya, Kiki, Kolya, Kotenokov, Butakov were there. Had tea at tennis. Went to Trina's played with granddaughter. Had dinner with Anastasia and Alexei.

5 Thursday. In the morning walked to the beach with Papa. At breakfast sat with Maltzev and Botkin. In the afternoon played tennis 4 with Papa, Mama, Anya, Kiki, Butakov, Zlebov and Pi were there. Had tea at tennis. Read in French. Had dinner with Anastasia and Alexei.

6 Friday. In the morning went to Yalta with Trina. At breakfast sat with the Frenchman[116] and Dedulin. In the afternoon played tennis 4 with Papa, Mama, Anya, Kiki, Pi, Butakov and Petrovsky were there. Had tea at tennis. Read in French. Had dinner with Anastasia and Alexei.

French lessons with Pierre Gilliard, "the Frenchman."

---

[116] Pierre Gilliard, French tutor for the imperial children.

7 Saturday. At breakfast sat with Prince Golitzyn and Smirnov. In the afternoon played tennis, Papa, Mama, we 4, Anya, Kiki, Kolya and Pi were there. Had tea at tennis. Went to vsenoshnaya and molebna. At dinner sat with Nilov and Prince Orlov.

8 Sunday. In the morning went with Mama and Alexei to molebna and obednya. At breakfast sat with the Governor and Nilov. In the afternoon sat with Mama and Anya on the balcony. Had tea 4 with Mama and Papa. Had dinner with Anastasia and Alexei.

9 Monday. In the morning had lessons and went to the beach. At breakfast sat with Uncle Georgiy and the Colonel. In the afternoon played tennis 4 with Papa, Mama, Anya, Kiki, Stolitza, Kolya and Pi were there. Had tea at tennis. At dinner in [illeg] room sat with Nilov and Zlebov. After that [we] danced and it was very merry.

Maria at an art lesson.

10 Tuesday. In the morning took a walk with Papa and went to the beach. At breakfast sat with Komarov and Nilov. In the afternoon played tennis 4 with Papa, Mama, Anya, Kiki, Kolya, Butakov and Kublitzky were there. Had tea at tennis. Read in French. Had dinner with Anastasia and Alexei.

At the beach.

11 Wednesday. Had lessons in the morning then went to
Yalta with Trina. Had breakfast 5 with Mama on the sofa.
In the afternoon chose things for the bazaar 4 with Mama,
ladies of the suite, Kiki, Kolya and [illeg] were there. Had
tea with same. Went to Trina's played with granddaughter.
Had dinner 4 with Mama on the sofa.

At the Yalta charity bazaar.

12 Thursday. In the morning read with Trina and met Papa who went to Kozmademyansky overnight. At breakfast sat with Botkin and Dedulin. In the afternoon walked 4 with Papa while Mama rode in a small carriage. Had tea 4 with Papa and Mama. Read in French. Had dinner with Anastasia and Alexei.

13 Friday. Had lessons in the morning. At breakfast sat with Gr. Apraksin and Nilov. In the afternoon 4 played [word crossed out] Pi and Anya while Mama was lying down with Kiki. Had [tea] with Papa and the same. Went to vsenoshnaya with Papa. Had dinner 4 with Papa and Mama on the sofa.

"4 with Papa and Mama."

14 Saturday. In the morning went to obednya with Papa. At breakfast sat with Lavrinovsky and Komarov. In the afternoon played tennis 4 with Papa, Mama, Anya, Kiki, Babitzyn, Kolya and Ippolit were there. Had tea in the little house. Went 4 to vsenoshnaya. At dinner sat with Apraksin and Nilov. Listened to Stefanesko.

The Romanov sisters picking mushrooms.

15 Sunday. In the morning we 4 went to obednya with Papa. At breakfast sat with Dedulin and Gr. Apraksin. In the afternoon went with Anastasia and Trina to Nina and Ksenia.[117] Had tea there, played croquet and swung on the giant steps. Had dinner with Anastasia and Alexei.

---

[117] Princesses Nina and Ksenia Georgievna, daughters of Grand Duke Georgiy Mikhailovich.

The Little Pair: Maria and Anastasia.

16 Monday. In the morning took a walk with Papa. Had
breakfast with Anastasia and Alexei and [illeg] Mama on the
sofa. In the afternoon Anastasia and I went to the beach
with Mama in a small carriage. Had tea with same. Went to
Yalta with Trina. Read in French. Had dinner with Anastasia
and Alexei with Mama on the sofa.

17 Tuesday. In the morning had lessons and went to the
beach with Trina. Had breakfast with Anastasia and Alexei
and Mama on the sofa. Kiki was here during the day. Olga
and Tatiana returned from Kozmademyansk with Papa.
Papa killed 1 deer. Had tea 4 with Mama and Papa.   Read
in French. Had dinner with Anastasia and Alexei.

18 Wednesday. In the morning took a walk with Papa and went to the beach. At breakfast sat with Dedulin and Apraksin. In the afternoon played tennis with Papa, Anya, Petrovsky, Kiki and Kolya were there. Had tea a lady with Mama and Trina [sic]. Read with Trina. Had dinner with Anastasia.

19 Thursday. In the morning had lessons. At breakfast sat with Uncle Georgiy and Prince Yusupov. In the afternoon tennis 4 with Papa. Mama, Anya, Kiki, Kolya and Bulgakov were there. Had tea in the little house. Read in French. Had dinner with Anastasia.

"4 with Papa..."

20 Friday. In the morning read with Trina. Had breakfast 5 with Mama on the sofa. In the afternoon we 4 took a walk with Mama in the small carriage. Had tea 4 with Mama. 4 rode to the People's House to set up things for the bazaar. Read with Trina. Had dinner 4 with Isa and Mama on the sofa.

21 Saturday. In the morning had lessons. Went to the beach with Trina. Had breakfast with Papa and Mama on the sofa. In the afternoon played tennis 4 with Papa, Mama, Anya, Kiki, [illeg] and Zlebov were there. Had tea at tennis. Went to vsenoshnaya. At dinner sat with Konsdadi... and Niko.

22 Sunday. In the morning went to a church consecration with Papa. Had breakfast 5 with Papa and Mama on the sofa. In the afternoon 5 with Mama went to the bazaar. Had dinner [illeg] I sat with Zelenetzky and Vikt. 4 in total were at the bazaar.

23 Monday. In the morning read with Trina. At breakfast sat with Apraksin and Nilov. In the afternoon 4 went to the bazaar. Had dinner with Papa and Mama on the sofa. Then again went to the bazaar.

24 Tuesday. In the morning had a lesson. At breakfast sat with [illeg]berg and Posolov. In the afternoon 4 went to the bazaar. Then played tennis with Papa, Mama, Anya, Kiki and Kolya were there. Had tea at tennis. Had dinner with

Papa and Mama on the sofa. Went to a concert 4 with Papa.

25 Wednesday. In the morning went to the beach with Trina. At breakfast sat with Sukhomlinov and Botkin. In the afternoon played tennis 4 with Papa, Mama, Anya, Kiki and Kolya. Had dinner 4 with Papa and Mama on the sofa. Had tea at tennis. Went to the circus with Papa. Vladimir Durov.[118]

26-27 September: blank

28 Saturday. Had a lesson in the morning. At breakfast sat with Shebeko and [illeg]. In the afternoon pasted in the album with Mama, Papa, Anya, Kolya, Kiki and Pi. Had tea 4 with Papa in Ai Todor at Aunt Ksenia's. Went to vsenoshnaya 4 with Papa. At dinner sat with Kaperov [illeg].

29 Sunday. In the morning went to obednya 4 with Papa. At breakfast sat with Gr. Apraksin and Dedulin. In the afternoon played tennis with Papa, Mama, Anya, Kiki, Kolya and Babitzyn were there. Had tea at home. Went 4 to vsenoshnaya [last sentence was crossed out]. Had dinner [crossed out] 4 with Papa and Mama with Anastasia and Alexei.

---

[118] The famous Durov circus

30 Monday. Had lessons in the morning. At breakfast sat with Gr. Apraksin and Maklakov. In the afternoon played tennis 4 with Papa, Mama, Kiki, Kolya and Anya were there. Had tea at home.   Went 4 to vsenoshnaya. Had dinner 4 with Papa and Mama on the sofa.

~

OCTOBER, 1913

1 Tuesday. In the morning 4 [the rest of entry is blank]

2 Wednesday. In the morning went to Yalta with Trina. At breakfast sat with Gr. Apraksin and [illeg]. In the afternoon played tennis with Papa, Mama, Anya, Kiki, Kublitzky and Kolya were there. Had tea at home. Read in French. Had dinner with Anastasia and Alexei.

3 Thursday. Had lessons in the morning. Went to Yalta with Trina. Had breakfast 5 with Mama. Played tennis 4 with Papa, Mama, Anya, Kiki and Kolya were there. Had tea with [illeg] and Papa. Read in French. Had dinner with Anastasia and Alexei.

With Anastasia in 1913.

4 Friday. Read in the morning. Went to a convoy parade. At breakfast sat with Dedulin and Grekov. In the afternoon played tennis 4 with Papa, Mama, Anya, Kiki, Kolya and Butakov were there. Had tea at home. Had dinner 4 with Papa and Mama on the sofa.

5 Saturday. In the morning went to a parade 5 with Mama and Papa. At breakfast sat with P[?] and Nikitin. In the afternoon 4 went to tennis with Papa, Mama, Anya, Kiki and Kolya. Had tea at home. Had dinner 4 with Papa and Mama on the sofa.

6 Sunday. In the morning went to obednya. At breakfast sat with Dumbadze and Botkin. In the afternoon went to tennis 4 with Mama, Papa, Anya, Kiki and Kolya. Had tea at

home. Went to Trina's. Had dinner with Anastasia and Alexei.

7 Monday. Had lessons in the morning. At breakfast sat with Grigorovich and Komarov. In the afternoon played tennis 4 with Papa. Mama, Anya, Kolya and Pi were there. Had tea at home. Read in French and in Russian. Had dinner with Anastasia and Alexei.

Maria and her sisters in October of 1913.

8 Tuesday. In the morning had lessons and were with Trina. At breakfast sat with Petrov and Nilov. In the afternoon played tennis 4 with Papa. Mama, Anya, Kiki and Kolya were there. Has tea 4 with Papa, Mama, Aunt Ksenia, Uncle Sandro and Irina. Read in Russian. Had dinner with Anastasia and Alexei.

9 Wednesday. In the morning went to Yalta with Trina and had lessons. At breakfast sat with Nikitin and Veselozorov. In the afternoon played tennis 4 with Papa. Mama, Kiki, Kolya, Shaprinsky and Shurik were there. Had tea at home. Read in Russian and in French. Had dinner with Anastasia and Mama on the sofa.

"Had tea at home."

10 Thursday. Had lessons in the morning. At breakfast sat with Knyazhevich and Nilov. In the afternoon drove to Ai Todor with Anastasia and Trina, played tennis and had tea, read in French.   Had dinner 4 with Papa and Mama on the sofa. Went to the Vladmir Durov Circus 4 with Papa.

11 Friday. On the morning went to the sea and church. Had breakfast 4 with Mama on the sofa. In the afternoon 4 played tennis, Mama, Anya, Kiki and Pi were there. Had tea with Papa and then at home. Read in French and in Russian. Had dinner with Anastasia.

12 Saturday. In the morning had lessons and went to the beach. At breakfast sat with Kasso and [space].   In the afternoon played tennis 4 with Papa. Mama, Anya, Kiki and Pi were there. Had tea at home. Went to vsenoshnaya 4 with Papa. At dinner sat with D[...] and Nilov.

13 Sunday. In the morning went to obednya 4 with Papa. At breakfast sat with Kochubei and the Governor. In the afternoon went with Anya [blank].

14 Monday. In the morning rode horses and had lessons. At breakfast sat with Dedgolinyn and Komorov. In the afternoon played tennis 4 with Papa.

"Rode horses." Maria and Tatiana on horseback.

15 Tuesday. In the morning had lessons and [went] to Yalta. At breakfast sat with Dedgolinyn and Botkin. In the afternoon 4 played tennis. Mama, Kiki, Kolya and Anya were there. Had tea with Papa and [illeg]. Read in Russian. Had dinner with Anastasia and Mama.

16 Wednesday. In the morning sat by the sea and had lessons. Had breakfast 5 with Mama on the sofa. In the afternoon 4 played tennis, Mama, Anya, Kiki, Kolya, Zborovsky and Shurik were there. Had tea with Papa at home and in between read in French and in Russian. Had dinner with Anastasia and Alexei.

17 Thursday. Had lessons in the morning and to the beach.
At breakfast sat with Nilov and Komarov. In the afternoon
played tennis 4 with Papa. Anya, Mama, Kiki, Butakov,
Shurik and Zborovsky were there. Had tea at home. Had
dinner with Anastasia and Alexei.

18 Friday. In the morning rode horses, had lessons. At
breakfast sat with Dedulin and Orlov. In the afternoon
played tennis 4 with Papa. Mama, Anya, Kiki, Kolya,
Shaprinsky and Zborovsky were there. Had tea at home.
Read in French and in Russian. Had dinner with Anastasia
and Alexei.

19 Saturday. In the morning had lessons and at the
beach. At breakfast sat with Komarov and Nilov. In the
afternoon played tennis 4 with Papa. Mama, Anya, Kiki,
Kolya and Babitzyn were there. Had tea at home. 4 went to
vsenoshnaya. Had dinner 4 with Papa and Mama on the
sofa.

20 Sunday. In the morning went to obednya with Papa.
Had breakfast 4 with Papa, Mama, Aunt Ksenia, Irina, Nikita,
Aunt Minnie[119] and Uncle Georgiy, Uncle Mitya and
Mamoyan. In the afternoon took a walk 4 with Papa and
Mama in a small carriage. Had tea with Papa and Mama.
Confession. Went to vsenoshnaya. Had dinner 4 with Papa
and Mama on the sofa.

---

[119] Grand Duchess Maria Georgievna, wife of Grand Duke Georgiy
Mikhailovich.

21 Monday. In the morning everyone took communion. Had breakfast 5 with Papa and Mama on the sofa. In the afternoon drove to Ai Todor with Anastasia and there [we] played and had tea. Went to vsenoshnaya. Had dinner 4 with Papa and Mama on the sofa.

22 Tuesday. In the morning [2 lines crossed out]. [...] with Maltzev and Dumbadze. In the afternoon took a walk with Papa, Kiki, Kolya, Shurik, Anya and Mama in a small carriage. Everyone had tea at home. Went with Malalo[illeg] [illeg]. Had dinner with Anastasia and Alexei.

23 Wednesday. In the morning rode horses. Had breakfast 5 with Prince Preuzbatsky and Mama. In the afternoon drove to Massandra[120] 4 with Papa, Anya, Isa, Nastenka, Pi, Ippolit and Kublitsky were there. Had tea 4 with Mama. Read in Russian and in French. Had dinner with Anastasia and Alexei.

24 Thursday. Had lessons in the morning. At breakfast sat with Dumbadze and Nilov. In the afternoon went to Ai Todor 4 with Papa and Mama and had tea there. Read in French. Had dinner with Anastasia and Alexei.

---

[120] The Massandra Palace had been built in the French chateau style by Count Vorontzov-Dashkov and was acquired by Emperor Alexander III in 1889, who hired architect Maximilian Messmacher. The Palace was finished in 1900. Prince Lev Galitzyn began the Massandra Winery in 1894, and the region was known for its delicious wines.

25 Friday. In the morning had lessons by the sea. Had breakfast with Mama, Alexei and Anastasia. In the afternoon rode horses with Anastasia, Nastenka and Isa to the [?]. Had tea 4 with Mama and Papa. Read in French. Had dinner with Papa and Mama on the sofa.

26 Saturday. Had lessons in the morning. At breakfast sat with Gulevich and Sazonov. Went to the bringing out of Desromt [?]. Had dinner with Papa and Mama on the sofa.

27 Sunday. In the morning went to obednya with Papa. At breakfast sat with Dumbadze and Knyazhevich. In the afternoon took a walk with Papa, Kiki, Kolya, Pi and Mama in a small carriage. Everyone had tea at home and also Aunt Ksenia. Read with Trina. Had dinner with Papa and Mama on the sofa.

28 Monday. In the morning went down to the beach and had lessons. At breakfast sat with Kamarov and Apraksin. In the afternoon [we] played tennis, Papa, Mama, Anya, Kiki, Kolya and Kublitsky were there. Had tea at home. Read in French. Had dinner with Anastasia.

29 Tuesday. In the morning went with Papa and Mama to Dedulin's sailing off. Had breakfast 5 with Mama and Papa. In the afternoon played tennis, Papa, Mama, Anya, Kiki and Kolya were there. Had tea at home. Read in Russian. Had dinner with Anastasia.

30 Wednesday. Took a walk in the morning and had lessons. At breakfast sat with Sazonov and Smirnov. In the afternoon played tennis, Papa, Mama, Anya, Kiki, Kolya [illeg] and Zborovsky were there. Had tea at home. Read in French and in Russian. Had dinner with Anastasia and Alexei.

31 Thursday. Had lessons in the morning. At breakfast sat with Orlov and Nilov. In the afternoon played tennis, Papa, Mama, Pi, Shurik, Zborovsky, Butakov and Anya were there. Had tea at home. Read in French. At dinner in the kayut-kompania [sat] with Kolya and [illeg]. After dinner there were [illeg] it was very merry.

~

NOVEMBER, 1913

1 Friday. In the morning went to Yalta and lessons. Sat with Sukhomlinov and Prince Trubetskoi. In the afternoon 4 played tennis, Mama, Papa, Kiki, Kolya, Anya, Zborovsky and Shurik were there. Had tea at home. Read in French and Russian. Had dinner with Anastasia and Alexei.

2 Saturday. Blank

3 Sunday. In the morning I was lying down and had breakfast lying down. In the afternoon stayed home. Had tea 4 with Mama, Papa, Kolya, Pi, Shurik, Zborovsky and Anya. At dinner on the yacht sat with Komarov and Nilov. After dinner sat, danced and had awfully lot of fun.

"... had awfully lot of fun."

4 Monday. In the morning had a lesson. At breakfast sat with Nilov and Botkin. In the afternoon 4 played tennis, Papa, Mama, Any, Kiki, Kolya, Pi and Zborovsky were there. Had tea at home and Christopher.[121] Read in French. Had dinner 4 with Papa and Mama on the sofa. Went to [illeg] with Papa.

5 Tuesday. In the morning had lessons. At breakfast sat with Papa and the Governor. In the afternoon pasted in albums with Mama, Kolya, Anya, Kiki, Pi and Stolitza. Had tea at home. Had dinner with Anastasia and Alexei.

---

[121] Prince Christopher of Greece and Denmark, brother of "Aunt Minnie."

6 Wednesday. Blank

7 Thursday. In the morning 4 with Papa toured the ship "Peter the Great" and stopped by the yacht. At breakfast sat with Uncle Georgiy and Komarov. In the afternoon played tennis 4 with Papa; Mama, Anya, Kiki, Pi, Shurik and Zborovsky were there. Had tea at home. Read in Russian. Had dinner with Anastasia.

8 Friday. In the morning went to Yalta and had lessons. At breakfast sat with the Commander of the 59th regiment [illeg]. In the afternoon 4 played tennis with Papa, Kiki, Mama, Pi, Shurik, Shaprinsky and Anya were there. Had tea at home. Read in French and Russian. Had dinner with Mama and Anastasia.

Maria and an officer on the tennis court.

9 Saturday. In the morning had lessons. At breakfast sat with Nilov and Kiki. In the afternoon 4 played tennis, Mama, Papa, Anya, Kiki, Shurik and Zborovsky were there. Had tea at home. Went 4 to vsenoshnaya. At dinner sat with Botkin and Count Fredericks.

10 Sunday. In the morning 4 with Papa to obednya. At breakfast sat with Nilov and Komarov. In the afternoon went to Kharax with Anastasia and Trina. Had tea there and played hide and seek. Had dinner with Anastasia and Alexei.

11 Monday. In the morning went to Yalta and had lessons. At breakfast sat with Botkin and Nilov. In the afternoon

played tennis, Papa, Mama, Anya, Kiki, Kolya, Shurik, Zborovsky and Sumarkov were there. Had tea at home. Read in French and Russian. Had dinner with Anastasia and Alexei.

12 Tuesday. Had lessons in the morning. At breakfast sat with Shurik and Nilov. In the afternoon 4 played tennis, Mama, Papa, Anya, Shurik and Kiki were there. Had tea at home. Read in French. Had dinner with Anastasia and Alexei.

13 Wednesday. In the morning went to Yalta. Lessons. At breakfast sat with Komarov and Nilov. In the afternoon 4 played tennis, Papa, Mama, Anya, Kiki, Kolya, Shurik and Zborovsky were there. Had tea at home. Read in French and Russian. Had dinner 4 with Papa and Mama on the sofa.

14 Thursday. In the morning went to moleben. At breakfast sat with Nilov and Komarov. In the afternoon took a walk with Papa, Anya, Kiki, Kolya, Shurik and Mama in equipage. Had tea at home. Went 5 with Mama and Papa to cinematograph. Had dinner with Anastasia and Alexei.

15 Friday. Had lessons in the morning in Yalta. At breakfast sat with Nilov and Botkin. In the afternoon took a walk with Papa, Anya, Kiki, Kolya, Pi and Mama in a carriage. Had tea at home. Read in Russian. Had dinner with Anastasia and Alexei.

16 Saturday. Had lessons in the morning. At breakfast sat with Nilov and Komarov. In the afternoon pasted in albums with Papa, Mama, Anya, Kiki, Pi, Nevirovsky, Zborovsky and Drenteln. Had tea at home. Went 4 with Papa to Asenovtzev's. At dinner sat with Nilov and Prince Trubetskoi.

17 Sunday. Blank

18 Monday. In the morning had lessons and took a walk. At breakfast sat with Nilov and Prince Trubetskoi. In the afternoon played tennis, Papa, Mama, Anya, Kiki, Kolya, Shurik, Zborovsky and Sumarkov were there. Had tea at home. Read in French and Russian. Had dinner with Anastasia and Alexei.

19 Tuesday. In the morning had lessons. Had breakfast 5 with Mama on the sofa. In the afternoon 4 took a walk with Kiki, Kolya, Shurik, Kotenok,[122] Anya and Mama in a carriage. Had tea at home with Papa. Read in French. Had dinner with Anastasia and Alexei.

20 Wednesday. In the morning went to Kastritsky's and had a lesson. At breakfast sat with Vetkin and Nilov. In the afternoon 4 played tennis, Papa, Mama, Anya, Kiki, Kolya, Shurik, Zborovsky and Sumarkov were there. Had tea at

---

[122] Literally means "kitten;" presumably Maria's nickname for Kotenkin.

home. Went 4 to vsenoshnaya. Had dinner 4 with Papa and Mama on the sofa.

21 Thursday. In the morning 4 went to obednya. At breakfast sat with Dumbadze, Kokovtzev. In the afternoon played tennis, Papa, Mama, Anya, Kiki, Butkov, Zborovsky and Sumarkov were there. Went to Trina's. Had dinner with Anastasia and Mama on the sofa.

22 Friday. In the morning went to Kastritsky's and had lessons. At breakfast sat with Prince Trubetskoi and Nilov. In the afternoon played tennis, Papa, Mama, Anya, Kiki, Kolya, Shurik, Zborovsky and Sumarkov were there. Had tea at home. Read in French and Russian. Had dinner with Anastasia and Alexei.

23 Saturday. Had lessons in the morning. At breakfast sat with Uncle Nikolasha[123] and Count Shtekelberg. In the afternoon 4 played tennis, Papa, Mama, Anya, Kiki, Kolya, Shurik, Zborovsky and Sumarkov were there. Had tea at home. Went 4 with Papa to vsenoshnaya. At dinner sat with Komarov and Nilov.

24 Sunday. In the morning 4 with Papa went to obednya. At breakfast sat with [illeg] and the Governor. In the afternoon 4 took a walk with Papa, Anya, Kiki, Kolya and Mama in a carriage. Had tea at the yacht, sat with Stolitza

---

[123] Grand Duke Nikolai Nikolaevich, the Tsar's cousin.

and Kublitsky. Went to Trina's. Had dinner with Anastasia and Alexei.

25 Monday. Had lessons in the morning. At breakfast sat with Orlov and Count Shtekelberg. In the afternoon played at home, 4, Papa, Mama, Anya, Kiki, Kublitsky and Kotenok were there. Had tea at home. Read in French and Russian. Had dinner with Anastasia and Mama on the sofa.

26 Tuesday. In the morning 5 [went] with Papa and Mama to a parade. At breakfast sat with Kachalov and Count T[illeg]. In the afternoon 4 took a walk with Papa, Anya, Kiki, Kolya, Babitzyn, Shurik and Mama in a carriage. Had tea at home. Read in French. Had dinner with Alexei and Anastasia. Had our hair washed.

27 Wednesday. In the morning went to Yalta and had lessons. At breakfast sat with Nilov and Count Apraksin. In the afternoon 4 played tennis, Papa, Mama, Anya, Kiki, Kolya, Shurik, Zborovsky and Sumarkov were there. Had tea at home. Read in French and Russian. Had dinner with Anastasia and Alexei.

28 Thursday. In the morning had lessons. At breakfast sat with Nilov and Komarov. In the afternoon 4 played at home, Papa, Mama, Anya, Kiki, Kotenok and Shurik were there. Had tea at home. Read in Russian. Had dinner with Anastasia and Alexei.

29 Friday. In the morning had lessons. At breakfast sat with Nilov and Prince Trubetskoi. In the afternoon 4 played at home, Papa, Mama, Anya, Kiki, Kolya, Shurik and Zborovsky were there. Had tea at home. Read in French and Russian. Had dinner 4 with Papa and Mama on the sofa. Went 4 with Papa to the theatre, "The Forgotten Outbuilding" and live pictures.

30 Saturday. Had lessons in the morning. Had breakfast 5 with Papa and Mama on the sofa. In the afternoon 4 played at home, Papa, Mama, Anya, Kiki, Kolya, Pi, [illeg] and Zborovsky were there. Had tea at home. Went 4 to vsenoshnaya. At dinner sat with Nilov and Komarov.

~

DECEMBER, 1913

1 Sunday. In the morning 4 went to obednya. At breakfast sat with Count Shtekelberg and the Governor. In the afternoon 4 played at home, Papa, Mama, Anya, Kiki, Kolya, Kotenok, Shurik and Zborovsky were there. Had tea at home. At dinner in the yacht's cabin [...]

2 Monday. In the morning went to Yalta and lessons. At breakfast sat with Nilov and Prince Trubetskoi. In the afternoon 4 played at home, Mama, Papa, Kiki, Kolya, Pi, Shurik, Anya and Zborovsky were there. Had tea at home. Read in French and Russian. Had dinner with Anastasia and Alexei.

3 Tuesday. In the morning had lessons. At breakfast sat with Nilov and Komarov. In the afternoon 4 played at home, Papa, Mama, Anya, Kiki, Kolya, Shurik, Zborovsky and Nevirovsky were there. Had tea at home. Read in French. Had dinner with Anastasia and Alexei.

4 Wednesday. In the morning went to Yalta and lessons. At breakfast sat with Nilov and Komarov. In the afternoon 4 took a walk and played at home, Mama, Papa, Anya, Kiki, Kublitsky, Shurik and Zborovsky were there. Had tea at home. Read in French and Russian. Had dinner with Anastasia and Alexei.

5 Thursday. Had lessons in the morning. At breakfast sat with Nilov and Prince Trubetskoi. In the afternoon 4 played at home, Mama, Papa, Anya, Kiki, Shurik, Zborovsky, Nevirovsky and Dmitri were there. Had tea at home. Went 4 to vsenoshnaya. Had dinner 4 with Papa, Dmitri and Mama on the sofa.

Maria looking through a spyglass.

6 Friday. In the morning 4 with Papa went to obednya. At breakfast sat with Grinv[illeg] and Ebergard. In the afternoon 4 played at home, Papa, Mama, Anya, Kiki, Shurik and Zborovsky were there. Had tea at home. At dinner in the cabin room sat with Nilov and Zlebov. After danced and played, it was merry.

7 Saturday. Had lessons in the morning. At breakfast sat with Dmitri and Count Shtekelberg. In the afternoon 4 played at home, Mama, Papa, Dmitri, Anya, Kiki, Kolya, Shurik and Zborovsky were there. Had tea at home. Went 4 to vsenoshnaya. At dinner sat with Dmitri and Count Shtekelberg.

144

8 Sunday. In the morning 4 with Papa went to obednya. At breakfast sat with Nilov and the Governor. In the afternoon 4 played at home, Mama, Papa, Anya, Dmitri, Kiki, Kolya, Shurik and Zborovsky were there. Had tea at home. Had dinner with Anya and Mama on the sofa.

9 Monday. Had lessons in the morning. At breakfast sat with Markhan Pasha and Count Apraksin. In the afternoon 4 played at home, Mama, Papa, Anya like, Dmitri, Kiki, Kublitsky, Shurik and Zborovsky were there. Read in Russian and French. Had dinner with Anastasia and Alexei.

10 Tuesday. In the morning had lessons. Had breakfast with Alexei, Anya and Mama on the sofa. In the afternoon sat with Mama. Had tea 4 with Papa, Mama and Dmitri. Read in French. Had dinner with Anastasia and Alexei.

"Breakfast with Alexei..."

11 Wednesday. In the morning had lessons. At breakfast sat with Komarov and Count Shtekelberg. In the afternoon 4 took a walk with Papa, Kiki, Kotenok, Zborovsky, Dmitri and Mama in a carriage. Had tea at home. Had dinner with Anastasia. Went 4 with Papa to vsenoshnaya.

12 Thursday. In the morning had lessons. At breakfast sat with Dmitri and Uchitel. In the afternoon played at home, Papa, Mama, Dmitri, Kiki, Pi, Shurik and Zborovsky were there. Had tea read in Russian. Had dinner with Anastasia.

13 Friday. In the morning had lessons. At breakfast sat with Dmitri and Count Apraksin. In the afternoon 4 played games, Papa, Mama, Kiki, Pi, Zborovsky, Zlebov and Dmitri were there. Had tea at home. Read in French and Russian. Had dinner with Anastasia.

14 Saturday. In the morning went to Yalta and lessons. At breakfast on "Kichkum" sat with Christopher. In the afternoon 4 took a walk with Papa, Kiki, Pi, Shurik, Zborovsky and Mama in a carriage. Had tea at home and also Dmitri. Read in French and Russian. Had dinner with Nastenka and Mama on the sofa.

15 Sunday. In the morning 4 with Papa went to obednya. At breakfast sat with Nilov and Dumbadze. In the afternoon 4 took a walk with Papa, Kiki, Kotenok, Zborovsky and Mama on the sofa [sic]. Had tea with Nina, Ksenia, Vasya and Nicky. Had dinner with Anastasia and Alexei.

16 Monday. Took a walk. At breakfast sat with Nilov and Count Apraksin. In the afternoon later went to Yalta. Had tea 4 with Papa, Mama, Dmitri and officers. Sat 4 with Pi, Kublitsky and K[illeg]. At dinner sat with Nilov and Botkin. Sat with P[illeg] Kolya.

17 Tuesday. In the morning arrived in Sevastopol. At breakfast sat with Nilov and Komarov. In the afternoon sat and talked with Pi, Kolya and Kotenok. Had tea 4 with Mama, Papa, ladies and officers. Sat with Kolya and looked at the train. There was a prayer service on the deck and

then we left the yacht to the train and it departed. It was very boring. At dinner sat with Nilov and Papa.

18 Wednesday. In the morning read with Trina. At breakfast sat with Papa and Ivanov. In the afternoon 4 sat at Mama's. Had tea 4 with Papa, Dmitri and the suite. Read with Trina. At dinner sat with Papa and Dmitri.

19 Thursday. In the morning 5 sat with Mama. At breakfast sat with Papa and Nilov. Read with Trina. Had tea 4 with Papa and the suite. Arrived in Tsarskoe Selo. Had dinner 4 with Papa, Mama, Grandmama, Aunt Ksenia, Aunt Olga, Irina and Dmitri.

Maria and her sisters with "Papa" and "Grandmama."

20 Friday. In the morning stayed at home. Had breakfast with Papa, Mama and Count Grabbe. In the afternoon all went to Znamenie,[124] then took a walk with Papa. Had tea 4 with Papa and Mama. Had dinner with Anya, Isa and Mama on the sofa.

21 Saturday. In the morning 4 skated. Had breakfast 5 with Papa, Mama, Aunt Olga, Uncle Boris, Count Fredericks, Count Sheremetiev, Anastasia and Alexei. Had tea 4 with Papa, Mama and Aunt Olga. Went to vsenoshnaya 4 with Papa and Aunt Olga. Had dinner 4 with Papa, Aunt Olga and Mama on the sofa.

22 Sunday. In the morning 4 went with Papa to the Kaspiisky parade. At breakfast sat with Uncle Nikolasha and Count M[illeg]. Took a walk with Papa. Had tea with Papa, Mama and Anastasia. Had dinner 4 with Papa and Mama on the sofa.

23 Monday. In the morning took a walk 4 with Trina. Had breakfast 5 with Papa, Mama and Mordvinov. In the afternoon set up for yolka. Had tea 4 with Papa and Mama. Had dinner with Anastasia and Alexei.

24 Tuesday. In the morning 4 went to obednya with Papa and Mama. Had breakfast 5 with Papa and Mama. In the afternoon gave out firs to all ladies and got some ourselves.

---

[124] Church at Tsarskoe Selo.

Had tea 4 with Papa, Mama and Anya. Went 4 with Papa to Grandmama's for yolka and vsenoshnaya and had dinner. Aunt Olga, Uncle Petya, Aunt Ksenia, Uncle Sandro and the children were there.

25 Wednesday. In the morning 5 went to obednya with Papa. Had breakfast 5 with Papa, Mama and Aunt Olga. Had tea 4 with Mama and Papa. Had dinner 4 with Papa and Mama on the sofa, also Aunt Olga.

26 Thursday. Had breakfast 5 with Papa, Mama and [illeg]. In the afternoon 5 went to convoy yolka with Papa and Aunt Olga, later the Cossacks danced lezginka.[125] Had tea 4 with Papa and Mama. Had dinner with Anastasia and Alexei.

27 Friday. In the morning 4 with Nastenka to the yolka at nanny school. Had breakfast 5 with Papa, Mama and Uncle Kostya. In the afternoon 4 took a walk. Had tea with Alexei and Anastasia. Went to Trina's. Had dinner with Anastasia and Alexei.

---

[125] Traditional dance from the Caucasus Mountains.

Contemporary postcard of the Nanny School at Tsarskoe Selo

28 Saturday. In the morning 5, Papa and Mama went to obednya. At breakfast sat with Delsaleti and Osipov. In the afternoon 4 went to Grandmama's and Aunt Olga's, had tea, played and had dinner. Irina, Ada, D[illeg], Felix, Sasha, mother, Kolya, Marie Clare, Dina, [illeg], Kulbnev, Kulikovsky, Petlitsa, Shurik, Victoria, Yegorov and [illeg].

29 Sunday. In the morning 4 took a walk. Had breakfast 5 with Papa, Mama and Aunt Mavra. Went to Grandmama's for officers' yolka and had tea 4 with Grandmama, Aunt Olga and Aunt Ksenia. Had dinner 4 with Papa and Mama on the sofa.

30 Monday. In the morning stayed at home. Had breakfast 5 with Papa, Mama, Aunt Olga and Uncle Petya. In the afternoon 4 took a walk with Papa and Aunt Olga. Had tea

151

4 with Papa and Aunt Olga. Had tea 4 with Papa, Mama and Aunt Olga. The same went to vsenoshnaya and had dinner.

31 Tuesday. In the morning 4 took a walk. Had breakfast 5 with Papa, Mama and Ioann. In the afternoon with Anastasia and Mama went to Znamenie and to the Sobor.[126] Had tea 4 with Papa, Mama and Anya. Went to Trina's. Had dinner 4 with Papa and Mama on the sofa.

Signed, "Maria."

---

[126] Feodorovsky Cathedral.

Other books from the "Romanovs In Their Own Words" series by Helen Azar

29626612R00095

Printed in Great Britain
by Amazon